SECRETS OF STEPPING WITH FAITH IN GOD

SECRETS OF STEPPING WITH FAITH IN GOD

Rachel—Author

Secrets of Stepping With Faith In God
Copyright © 2013 Rachel

All rights reserved in cooperation with and compliance to the United States Copyright Act of 1976 as currently revised whereby any reproduction, whether by mechanical, electronic, audio or visual methods is prohibited except by written consent of the publisher. Brief quotes as specified in the United States Copyright Act of 1976 as currently revised are excepted.

Scriptures, unless otherwise noted, are taken from The King James Version of the Holy Bible, used with permission.

All emphasis added to Scripture are at the discretion of the author. TMN/Wisdom Merchants Publishing style capitalizes nouns and pronouns that refer to God, Lord, Holy Spirit, Father, and/or Son. Also note, we choose to not capitalize the name satan and/or various related terms signifying his name.

Cover photo and design
Copyright © 2013 Velma Crow

ISBN-10:0989473570
ISBN-13:978-0989473576

DEDICATION

This book is dedicated to my sons,
Jeffrey, Craig, and Mark

TABLE OF CONTENTS

A RESTING PLACE	185
ANGER	81
ANXIETY	42
ATTITUDE	75
AUTHORITY	38
BALANCE	34
BEGINNINGS	13
CHANGE	116
CHEERFULNESS	214
CONTENTMENT	190
CORRECTION	197
COVENANT	99
CREDIBILITY	53
DECEPTION PART 1	32
DECEPTION PART 2	126
DECISIONS	17
DREAMS	147
DUPLICITY	139
ENCOURAGEMENT	36
ETHICS	73
ETIQUETTE	87
EXPECTATIONS	1
FAITHFULNESS	132
FEELINGS	47
FORERUNNER	156
FORGIVENESS—THE ROAD TO THE HAPPY LIFE	164
FREEDOM	84
FRIEND?	97
FRIENDSHIP	170

FRUITS OR NUTS?	220
GRATITUDE	172
HARVEST	70
HONOR	57
HOPE	200
IDOLS	22
IMAGINATION	129
INCREASE	224
INSPIRATIONS	107
INTERESTS	51
INTIMACY WITH THE FATHER	92
INTIMIDATION	28
IS IT FAITH? PART 1	203
IS IT FAITH? PART 2	205
KINDNESS	153
LAUGHTER	141
LOVE	159
MERCY	193
MOTIVATION	94
OCCUPATION	101
OUR BREAD	137
PEACE Part 1	65
PEACE Part 2	110
PERFORMANCE: CURTAIN CALL	24
PERSEVERENCE	208
PLACE	150
PLANS	67
PRAYER	118
PRESUMING	217
PROCESS	49
PROTOCOL	45
PURPOSE	3

RECEIVING	123
REFLECTION	78
RESPECT	40
RESTITUTION	161
RESTORATION	5
REVELATION	30
SACRIFICE	104
SALVATION	59
SECURITY	175
SELF-EFACEMENT	188
SIIMPLICITY	121
SORROW	63
SURPRISES!!!	9
THE CUP: THE PRAYER	135
THE GODMATE	178
THE HIGHER LIFE	15
THE INTERCESSOR	167
THE KINGDOM LIFE	89
THE WEAKER VESSEL	227
THOUGHT CONTROL	211
TIMING	182
TITHES	55
TRANSITIONS	26
TRIUMPH	61
UNDERSTANDING	113
VICTORIOUS	11
WINNER . . . YES . . . YOU!	20
WONDER	7
WORDS	144
WORKS OF FLESH	222
ABOUT THE AUTHOR	231

ACKNOWLEDGMENTS

This book cannot be published without acknowledging the source of my strength and my teacher:

My Lord Jesus Christ has given me strength to overcome and take the next step in life, even when I couldn't see the place to set my foot for that next step.

Holy Spirit has been my Teacher, my Comforter, and my Guide throughout my life. Thank You, Holy Spirit for giving me directions for living and enabling me to put those directions into teachings so others can benefit through what You've done in me.

I must honor my earthly mentor, Dr. Mike Murdock, whose teachings on these subjects opened the door for me to do the impossible—something I could not imagine—publishing this book. Thank you Dr. Murdock for your faithfulness to your call, seeking out and establishing wisdom.

EXPECTATIONS

What are you expecting today?
Is it something you thought of yourself?
Is it what God has shown you?
Has it been confirmed from the mouth of two or three witnesses?

These are some of the questions we must ask ourselves that, with the answers being in Christ Jesus, enable us to answer more intelligently. The question today is what are you expecting today?

God said if we would open our mouth that He would fill it. Faith in God and His promises to you will birth expectation. Expectation not birthed from the leading of the Holy Spirit will leave you disappointed every time.

Set your sights on things above. Refuse to accept anything that God did not say. Do accept what He said to you, for He is truth and He is not a man that He should lie.

The Psalmist and King David said this in Ps.62:5: *My soul wait thou only upon God, for my expectation is from Him*! Therefore my friend do not cast away your confidence and faith in God that is founded on our Mighty God and His strength, His Word. You will not be disappointed, but will receive what He has told you to expect.

Cast not away your confidence,
*which has great recompense of **reward**!*
Hebrews 10:35

PURPOSE

What is your purpose for living?
What is God's purpose for you on this earth?
Have you discovered it?
Are you chasing your passion and/or your purpose?

Many have found their purpose and still enjoy some of their passions. Passion will follow purpose—once you find it.

God tells us in Ecclesiastes 3:1, that there is a purpose, a time, that He planned for you—"out loud and on purpose!"

Seek God and His holiness. Follow His plan for that is the road that will lead you to your purpose. Keep going until you discover it and great will be your joy—great will be your fulfillment.

God says, "I know why I created you...I know what I planned for you." When God imagines...it is already done!

Jeremiah 29:11, tells us, *I know the thoughts that I think toward you, says the Lord, thoughts of peace and not of evil, to give you a future and a hope!!!"*

Trust in God. He will bring you to it!!!

Purpose is the true reason for you and me being created. We are all a part of God's plan. Our lives and our purpose fit beautifully into His plan of redeeming the world back to Himself. Our personality, even our physical design has a purpose in the plan God has for us. Being in our appointed place, doing our purpose makes everyday life an achievement instead of a chore.

We tend to dread what we are doing, what we label as work or a career until we find our purpose—then—OH! THEN!!! "Work" becomes a joy! It fulfills us and we begin to see the pieces of the once hidden parts of our lives start to fit together to make a big and beautiful picture of what God was planning for us to do when He made us!!!

We must fight hard for our purpose, not physically, but spiritually, and sometimes emotionally, then adding physical strength to reach our purpose. When we discover our purpose and start fulfilling it—we realize it is not just our obedience to God—it is also being true to ourselves.

This is where we find ourselves being outstanding in all we do. No one can do what we do. No one can compete with us. Not NOW! Not in our purpose for no one can compete with God's design!

Find your joy.
Find your true happiness in your life's work.
FIND GOD!
To everything there is a season,
And a time for every purpose
Under heaven.
Ecclesiastes 3:1

RESTORATION

What is it, concerning your life, that needs restoration?

- Finances
- Relationships
- Marriage
- Credit
- Health
- Employment

These are just some of the things where restoration becomes a desire.

If you are walking in obedience with God, He can restore all of these things. It depends on you. God is ready and willing, today, to do these things for us!

You must have trust in God and His Word. God can make these things happen as you seek Him for wisdom of how to use the knowledge you have—old or new. He will surely do it, but indeed you must fulfill your part. Double for your trouble is the least amount you will ever receive in godly restoration.

Study the book of Job. Job was restored with double.

There is a secret to receiving His promises on this. It is keeping your faith and trust in God and His word. Whatever it looks like, it is not bigger than God!

Make holiness before a Holy God your goal. God does require truth in the innermost being. Restoration, actually means it is now better than before, better than the original.

Whatever it is I know our God is able to do it! He has done it for me and He will do it for you. Yes! He will do it again! Psalm 37:3-4 tells us:

Trust in the Lord, and do good: Dwell in the land, and FEED on his faithfulness. Delight yourself also in the Lord, and He will give you the desires of your heart! (Emphasis added)

Start believing him today.
Never quit!
And He will start restoring you today!!!

WONDER

Did you ever sit and wonder—as you gaze into space—about God—yourself—others—or—just things?

It is a good thing to wonder. It seems to expand the mind—to ponder the amazing things that defy our imagination. To contemplate the things of wonder that cause smiles to come creeping across our face and laughter to erupt from our hearts adds dimension to our souls and refreshes our spirit!

When we just see some of the depths of our God, He quickly becomes the greatest wonder of them all. A greater wonder than man's "wonders of the world." He is truly a mighty God! The Man—Jesus—Who is our God, owns no obvious end to His creative abilities. *He is before all things and in Him all things consist*—Colossians 1:17!

This kind of wonder, and it is a God wonder, inspires us to think more, think deeper, feel with greater sensitivity. This kind of wonder inspires us to wonder, "What else is it in me that I have yet to discover,"…for there is no end of God.

There is no end of the God in me! The wonder of Him,

and Him in me! To us (saints), *God willed to make known what are the riches of the glory of this mystery among the gentiles, which is Christ in you the hope of Glory—* Colossians 1:27!

A wonder to ponder today!!!

SURPRISES!!!

Do you like good surprises?
Ever wished you could surprise someone who was least expecting it?
Did you?
Was it fun?

I am sure you have been surprised by some great things <u>sometime</u> in your lifetime! You probably remember exactly how it went—how it made you feel. Good surprises create great memories. Everyone gets surprised at some point in time, and many times it is a wonderful thing.

Let's think about good things, good surprises. Most surprises are things you could not, and did not help create for yourself. Good surprises cause you great excitement and diversified reactions from others. If we keep our priorities right, guard our friendships, and live by the principles of God's word then we can expect a greater amount of great surprises to come our way.

Even a "not so good surprise" summons Jesus to our side—sometimes to our surprise. We can then allow Him to carry that weight. I think God planned many surprises for us. He blesses the prepared mind—the expectant mind!

He has always done things no man would ever have dreamed possible! God has no bad surprises in His hands for us. If we live by His principles we know His promises are all good!

God loves laughter, He created it! He is joy! God has many wonderful surprises still in store for you! The ones that appear to be "not so good", they too will work out for your good because you love Jesus and you are called by Him!

But as it is written: Eye has not seen nor ear heard, nor have entered into the heart of man the things which God has prepared for those who love him!" 1 Corinthians 2:9.

Think on this...
surprises you never dreamed possible,
just for you!!!
God is for you, not against you,
forever more!!!

VICTORIOUS

Victory—sometimes we forget
and we began thinking, "Is it ever coming?"
Will I live to see it?
Is it meant for me?

I have good news today! The answers to all these questions is, "YES!"

You already have the victory! That is what Jesus was saying when He said, "*It is finished*!" He died to bury defeat and rose to ultimate victory.

Victory over ALL things!

We think we are warring for victory, but it is only over our flesh that we war! What are we learning in this battle? God has already given us the victory. He has already fought the battle, paid the price, and it is ours today! All we have to do is believe it, and start living a lifestyle of praise to Him as we continue to walk out this great truth!

We are simply walking out what Christ Jesus already did for us!

Today, you reign with Him! He is not defeated! He lives today, in you, therefore you are not defeated! He lives today. He loves today! He is watching you as you walk it out. He watches with encouragement, with intercession for you!

You are not alone and the good news is, you already have the victory! Get that revelation in your heart today! "It is finished!" Now, just finish walking it out. You will see where you are today…

He raised us up together, and made us to sit in the heavenly places in Christ Jesus!!! Ephesians 2:6.

We share in a partnership with Christ Jesus.
We sit where He sits.
We reign where He reigns…In ALL things.
In ALL dominion!!!

PRAISE HIM TODAY!!!

BEGINNINGS

There will be many times that we look for a beginning or a new beginning!
Ever wondered when or if a person, a thing—an event was ever going to begin?

When the answer does come, it will be a beginning. It can be a new beginning—new, fresh knowledge, a new status or position, a new relationship, a new life.

Many times we feel like a beginner with no experience when we set out on a new beginning. A new beginning is the grace of God giving us a new opportunity to begin again!

With God, we can begin again after failure and disappointment have been experienced. A beginning is the first part of what will unfold for us. If we start in obedience to God what unfolds is His will—His plan.

What begins well, ends well. What is begun in the flesh ends in the flesh. What is begun in the Holy Spirit can always remain in the Holy Spirit.

This is our decision. God is our beginning, our source

of real life and a real and new beginning.

Beginning is the first step in the endeavor, the work, commitment, marriage. If we are careful about our beginnings, then the result will always be positive. How we begin and the results depend on the quality of our decision of what, when, where, and how we begin.

Beginning is the first step. Plans and all our good intentions are never realized without our decision to begin. From the start, from the beginning, it can be His word manifesting and remaining—doing His work in and through us. Some have never experienced real, lasting beginnings for they have not embraced the fear of God which is the beginning of wisdom. Wisdom is a completer—a finisher. Therefore, though they begin many things, without wisdom, there is no true beginning with an expected end.

God has been careful to reveal to us the importance of "the fear of the Lord" in relation to wisdom. He mentions this in six different passages of scripture including, Psalm 111:10 which tells us the fear of God is the beginning of our wisdom.

Today really is the beginning of the rest of our lives. I pray for you it has begun with God, if so, great is the end! Only with God can we begin great and the end will then also be great! Let's do a wise thing and in this new beginning—as God did—as God is—Genesis, meaning "beginning," start with Him.

God is doing a new thing today, in your life. It begins today with His creation of the supernatural life! Get excited! Thank God for the new beginning! Start today, and that will be the beginning of a new life of faith and trust in God!

Believe Him!
Trust Him!
He loves you!!!

THE HIGHER LIFE

Have you ever considered the fact that God created the seed for sustaining life before He created man?

Then God said, Let the earth bring forth grass, the herb that yields seed and the fruit tree that yields fruit according to its kind, whose seed is in itself and it was so!—Genesis 1:11

God placed food on the earth in preparation to sustain the soon to come creatures including mankind, for whom it was created. He loved His creation and made provision for the sustenance of life. Even the death of things on earth provides for continuance of creation.

Life is sustained by the seed. Plants and animals spring forth from and are seeds, servants to man in many ways. The most significant of these is providing oxygen and food. "Everything is a seed," Dr. Murdock often speaks.

Plants and animals are seeds for our harvest of physical life. They nourish us, and cause growth and development. They sustain our health and life. If the plants and animals are not harvested they cannot feed man. Lower life must give way to produce the higher life, a Kingdom of God reward.

So it is that God's Word is the seed that nourishes us and produces spiritual life in us. In the Kingdom of God that which is lower serves and is the seed for transformation into a higher life. We take the seeds (provisions), of plants and animals and they become the substance of our physical life. 2 Corinthians 9:10 tells us that He not only supplies seeds but also bread for food.

We take the seed, the Word—Jesus, into our heart and that seed produces a Holy and spiritual life. He is spirit and truth! When His seed is sown into our heart then man truly does become a living soul. It has now become the higher life.

The seed is the word of God. Jesus was the Son that God allowed to be planted as a seed. That seed is still in the "now!" *And so it is written, the first man Adam became a living being. The last Adam became a life giving spirit!*—1 Corinthians15:45. He is the higher life! Allow him to sow the higher life into your heart today! He can! He will! He loves you!

Reach until you are infused with
the Kingdom of God
and heaven!!!

DECISIONS

Who likes to make decisions?
Do you?

Some people do not like making decisions! You just made one! You decided to read this teaching. Life is a series of daily decisions, some great and serious, others of less significance! Decisions have created our lifestyle and all the things around us! Now, that thought can make us look seriously at the significance of our decisions for sure!

I believe the most significant, the most beneficial thing a parent will ever teach a child is all about decisions—the consequences, the rewards, the timing, etc. Ever wished someone would have taught you this when you were very young?

No decision—many times—is a decision! Goodly discretion evolves to become decisions. Godly decisions will always be right decisions.

Dr. Mike Murdock was told by the Holy Spirit that "Decisions decide your wealth!" Think about that! Why we make a particular decision is oft times as significant or more significant than the decision itself!

Today we must recognize that we are at this time and place of life right now because of the sum total of all the decisions we ever made. One day, that will also be true when we stand in the judgment of the mighty God.

The longer we wait to make the decision to obey God, the older we will be when we start making right decisions that determine the quality of our life. All decisions carry a consequence! We must seek the Holy Spirit in order to make the right decisions. With our decisions made, we then pay with our lives in grief or great goodness as a result of them.

There will always be two ships in our life, representing what our choice is. Luke 5:1-11 teaches us about this. Read it today! Jesus will always be in the godly decision, the right boat!

There will always be nets; those are our circumstances. Sometimes, (Psalm 42:7), the waves of our circumstances try to take us under! We use our nets for fishing, trying to find the right place to locate fish—what we want, what we will receive.

Decisions! Yes, how we get what we want, and from whom we receive what we want is very significant. It must be a choice from Holy Spirit.

The higher the number of right decisions we make, the easier it becomes to make more right decisions. Each right decision makes us stronger in God and more confident within ourselves. Right decisions create great circumstances, great catches, great rewards! Our choices today decide where we abide tomorrow, heaven or hell. We will take nothing with us except what we have become.

Make good decisions today with the Holy Spirit. Get into the right boat, it's the one Jesus is sitting in. He is the Son of Man, the Lamb of God, our Shepherd!

For the Lamb of God who is in the midst of the throne will shepherd them and lead them into living waters, and God will wipe away every tear from their eyes.—Revelation 7:15.

Godly decisions today birth great tomorrows! You will ride above all circumstances when you and Jesus are in the same boat! Great will be your peace on the ocean of life!!! People who make right decisions are people who carry the spirit of peace.

To him who overcomes, I will grant to sit with me on my throne as I overcame and sat down with my Father on His throne.—Revelation 3:21.

There is hope for you—hope for your life to change, your finances to change, health to change. Right decisions birth these changes. There is still time to start making right decisions! Make the best one today...decide to obey Christ today. You can then overcome all!!!

Jump into the right boat and sail the sea of peace!!!
TODAY!!!

WINNER...YES...YOU!

You are a winner today!!!
Let me confirm that!

A winner is one who wins the race, accepts the challenge, and receives the reward!

Have you seen yourself as a winner? God sees you as a winner! There is no one that God created to become a loser. That is man's creation. We simply embrace a challenging but very rewarding lifestyle to become the real winner! Winners are simply people who refuse to "settle" for less. They each know that settling will not get them to the finish line, it will not make them the winner.

Paul said he would buffet his flesh into submission to his will to do his best for Christ and his mission. Winners refuse to listen to negative words. The words "no," "can't," "won't", etc. are not part of their vocabulary. A winner is proof that taking the high road each time we speak, each time we act, is the runway of the winner.

Everyone is on a runway sometime in their life. **Power** never stays forever in the same place except with the power of God. The one who wins is the one who refuses to stay where he finds himself and the challenge. Rosa Parks refused to stay with the ones who were "settling". Sir Winston Church Hill won great victories because he refused to quit! The true winner believes in God and in himself.

Many run the race to win but don't watch the score board—the promises of God—timing. They quit just before the victory bells rings. There is great celebration on earth for earthly winners, so imagine the celebrations in heaven for the winners!!!

The God of the universe, the Master of all things, all peoples, said *I am with you always*! He has never been intimidated, never lost a battle, and He is continually with us!

Paul is waiting to celebrate you! 2 Timothy 4:7: *I have fought the good fight, I have finished the race, I have kept the faith.*

These can be your words!
Isn't that exciting?!
Know you can plan on winning today!!!

IDOLS

What is an idol?
How do we know when we have an idol?
How do we get rid of idols?

Those who have NO idols are the ones who hold God as #1!

God is moving toward us and He has the desires of our heart in His hands! Psalm 37 gives us the key: *Delight yourself in the Lord, and he will give you the desires of your heart.*

May I remind you...God's word is truth. It's God talking. He is not a man that He would lie. He was also speaking when He gave us His commandments! If He is not #1, then the other nine commandments lose their significance altogether. If He is #1, His commandments become natural outgrowths of our relationship.

Delight is when something or somebody is the greatest joy, the thing that gives us the greatest pleasure. The only way God can be our joy and great pleasure is if He is our God and our <u>only</u> God.

An idol is a thing, somebody, a belief, even a child that we place before God and His plan for our life. It can be a pet, tradition, beliefs, even a deception. Any idol will cause you to lose the blessings of God and keep you from receiving the desires of your heart.

Throw all idols out of your heart today, tell Jesus He is going to be #1 from this day forth! Let Him hear you declare this. Let Him see it in your life. He wants to be #1 in your life. He is a jealous God! He wants to bring you that desire of your heart, but you hold the key!

Thou shalt have no other God's before me.

Live with Him #1 every day and then you will receive every day like as though you are #1 in God's heart as well!!!

Thou shalt love the Lord thy God with all thy heart, and with all thy soul, and with all they mind, and with all thy strength.
Mark 10:30

PERFORMANCE: CURTAIN CALL

Did you ever stop to think…
your life is really a public performance
each and every day?

Life is the constant display of one's thoughts, words, and deeds. When I look at your audience I then know for whom you are performing. If you don't know for whom you are performing it is quiet easy to discover! Ask yourself this question; your answer will reveal your audience:

If you were going to receive a very high honor, who would you want to be present to see you receive it?

That is who you are performing for in your heart, that is the audience you love.

Are you carrying out God's script or are you performing?

Is your performance for man or for God?

Is it an act and you are only an actor or is it real and from your heart?

If you are real, your performance will remain the same day after day. The title to your "Broadway Show," (since it is seen each day as on Broadway), will be titled by the name of your daily performance!

What is that one word that best describes you?
- Faithfulness?
- Credibility?
- Trustworthy?
- Warrior?

You may think only you know, but this is not true. Everyone watching your performance years before, one week ago…or today can name your show! Is it a sensation, long running, worth our applause, an award, recognition, the overcomers crown? Paul said in 2 Corinthians 11:6, he had been manifested among them in many things!

Its "curtain call" now, for God wants to show Himself strong and powerful! What is the name of your show, or is it God's show? Name it today and get started performing it every single day! You can be a movie star for God and His glory!

My speech, my preaching were not with persuasive words of human wisdom, but in demonstration of the spirit and of power, that your faith should not be in the wisdom of men, but in the power of God!—1 Corinthians 2:4-5!

Its curtain call for your life today!!!

ACT NOW!!!

TRANSITIONS

Are you in one?
It can be from one season to another, but it is transition!
It can be as simple as changing the key for the music or as drastic as becoming unemployed.
Some transitions come to us unexpectedly!

Transitions are simply the passings from one thing or one activity to another. Going from single to married, employed to unemployed, married to divorced, etc. All of these are transitions.

We must be vigilant, seeking counsel, guarding our affections, seeking wisdom! Transition brings with it many questions and the need to make important decisions. We must recognize when we have come into a transition! There are a few questions that must be addressed. For example: What is it that we will carry with us into this next season and what is it we leave behind? Transition is the time we experience the greatest need for our secret place!

When we seek God, He will give us answers, directions! This will slow our decision making, clear our vision, make us wait, then stability will come with God's answers to us!

Recognize the need for Godly wisdom and counseling for therein lies answers from God! Never rush or allow someone else to rush you, for God is not in rushing, He has no need to hurry. Yet, He's never late. Follow the path of peace! Be cautious for wisdom speaks and tells us, this is the place of our greatest mistakes.

Moses knew this! Leaders must know these things to lead properly and successfully. *My presence will go with you, and I will give you rest.* Moses asked God, "Show me thy way!" He said to God, *If your presence does not go with us, do not bring us up from here!"* Exodus 33:14-15.

Follow God's Word, His path of peace, and find that peace and rest!!! It will be His presence with you!!! Praise Him for His candle that lights your way in these times!!!

> You can make all quality decisions,
> not mistakes…
> Today!!!

INTIMIDATION

Somewhere, someone is frustrated today from intimidation. Is it you?

God has already spoken and said, *Ye shall not fear them, for the Lord your God, he shall fight for you* (Deuteronomy 3:22). Intimidation is simply doubting God; and what He said here.

You need to study to make sure—pray to be certain it is correct and it is from God. Then—trust in God!

When you are intimidated you are in fear to do or say what is right! It is fear that He will not be there for you when you "step out," either with a word or an act. There are many bullies in the world whose goal it is to intimidate others, satan is one of them. When this happens, you LET them win!

Going forth without any intimidation proves the bully, satan, to be the coward that he is. If you do not prove him to be the coward, he will prove you are the coward!

You are not a coward, but that is what the enemy wants to make you feel like and look like! You are The

Kings child! Take heart! Choose trust in God!

Entertaining a habit of hesitation can develop into the full blown spirit of intimidation! When you start seeing the enemy for what he is, your fear gives way to more confidence and trust in God. The God in you is great, but satan does not want the world to see that, OR YOU!

God is with you, never leaves you, and He wants to prove it to you! He cannot show Himself mighty and strong if you do not give Him the trust that affords Him that opportunity! David said, *The Lord is on MY side, I will not fear. What can man do to me*?--Psalm 118:6.

You must recognize God is right beside you. You need not fear! When you KNOW this, you will be set free from intimidation. Your faith will laugh in the face of fear! The God in you wants to show out! Let Him and receive your greater future today! The next time God gives you an opportunity to trust Him…give Him one to show Himself mighty on your behalf!!!

You can and He will!!!
Believe it today!
Receive it today!!!
It is truth!

REVELATION

Yes!
Exciting…Revelation!
Revelations!
God's disclosure of Himself to a man!

Powerful thought there!

Jesus knows when His Father has revealed Himself to a man: *Simon Peter Replied, You are the Christ, the Son of the Living God! Then Jesus answered him, Blessed are you Simon Bar-Jonah, for flesh and blood, (men), have not revealed this to you, but My Father who is in heaven!"* Matthew 16:16-17.

We can reveal the Christ, the Anointed One, in us, by His gifts and His fruits in us! However, we cannot see the Father's heart unless He reveals it to us Himself. No one can minister Jesus really without seeing Him; the true revelation of Himself. Revelation of Jesus comes to us as His word in us increases, for He is THE WORD! Jesus' life revealed Him as the Son of Man! Jesus birth into this world gave us the first revelation of our Father: God is love!

It was so great a gift OF love that He came into this

world heralded by a host of angels! They sang the explanation of His coming! The revelation of love...come down to rescue men from everything that is not love! Joy, Oh Joy!!!

Celebrate Christ birth for it is the revelation of God's love!! There is no greater revelation than the revelation of Christ, the Anointed One! Jesus came as a man to reveal His Father, and if you have seen Him, you have seen our Father. His Father's goal for Him now is for revelation of Him as King to be our revelation.

He wrote the vision. He wrote the book. It is called Revelation. Revelation is the unveiling and presentation of the King of Kings and Lord of Lords! HE IS! HE IS! HE IS!!!

If He is your Lord today, then He has become your King and must rule in your life today. Everything then becomes possible! You can have that revelation! He reigns in PURE LOVE.

Receive His love today, ALL of it!!! He will give you the revelation of who He is...LOVE. He already paid the price for you to love Him. Place Him on the throne of your heart today and let the King of Kings rule your life.

It will then be revelation after revelation
for there is no end to our King!

DECEPTION

Deception is simply believing a lie.

If satan can get you to believe a lie he can derail all your blessings and steal from you at the same time.

The reason God hates liars is because of His love for His people. He wants you never to believe a lie. He has put His Word, His wisdom, all around you to keep you safe!

When you believe a lie you have embarked on the path of your destruction. This path affects you, yourself, others around you, and also those who follow you. If there is a worst deception of them all, it would be that of deceiving ourselves, believing our own lie to ourselves.

A true friend is the one who will confront the deception in you. Who can receive this correction? The answer is: very few! Deceiving oneself grows thru imagination and develops then without a boundary. It remains only imagination. It becomes much easier because of sin's hold to believe the lie than to believe God's truth, or to face the truth.

When one is believing a lie it renders him too weak,

too blind, to ask the right question directed to the honest person or to God. The truth so desperately needed is that answer. Freedom from deceit is found in that honest answer. Those who continue to deceive themselves do not know themselves. Jeremiah 17:9, tells us this heart is desperately wicked.

Truth not received is destiny delayed. Know the truth and it makes you free. Free to pursue more truth and the true plan God has for your life.

A person who knows you are believing a lie and does not confront you does not love you. Those who do not want to hear the truth are not of God. *He that is of God heareth God's words: ye therefore hear them not, because you are not of God* John 8:47. Pursue truth today and you will find God and righteousness! Pray this prayer that David prayed from his honest heart…

Search me, Oh God, and know my heart, see if there is any wicked way in me, and lead me in the way everlasting!—Psalm 139:23.

You can be free of deception in one moment of honesty before God!!!

Free indeed…and right now!!!

BALANCE

How much thought do you or anyone you know
ever give to the word balance?

God gave that word some meaning!

*Let me be weighed in an even balance,
that God may know mine integrity.*
Job 31:6

If you are equal to something you are balanced. Christian balance is balanced alignment with God's principles.

God weighs everything for balance. For every negative thing there is a positive thing. There are many kinds of balances. There is balanced diet affording proper nutrition. There's the balance of power between governing bodies. There is balance of trade; the difference in exports and imports. Balance sheets tell us of our profit and loss.

When our life or part of our life is out of control, we are off balance in that area. It has become an extreme, not a balance. Perhaps with a weight gain a decision is made immediately to "crash diet." This an extreme. Upon hearing wisdom and wanting to correct sometimes we get off balance. For example, this Wisdom Key: "Silence cannot be misquoted" (Dr. Mike Murdock). Someone who really has something to say upon hearing this, may suddenly decide to say nothing. This is off balance.

Sudden excitement can cause us to react in an extreme act or word. A man who attempts to stop a habit of exaggeration and lying may start telling "too much truth," (using no discretion and exposing his personal life or the lives of others). This one has become off balance.

Weigh change and see if it is a balanced change. Most always in our attempt to correct, we get into the extremes. Over correction causes accidents! Practicing and entertaining sin is off balance with God's standards.

God said to one king, *You have been weighed in the balance and found wanting*—Daniel 5:27. Through presumptuous pride and brazen irreverence, Belshazzar failed to acknowledge God's ultimate Lordship on the earth, and therefore over Babylon. God weighs people and things! He evaluated Belshazzar and found him deficient!

Who has measured the waters in the hollow of his hand, and meted out heaven with the span, and comprehended the dust of the earth in a measure, and weighted the mountains in scales, and the hills in a balance?—Isaiah 40:12.

God and His word are weighing us today.
Has He found you balanced or wanting?
I have good news for you!
You can become balanced today with God and His Word!!!

Just believe it and do it!

ENCOURAGEMENT

Do you need encouragement today?

When the battle is of God, your victory is a sure thing! He is the undefeated God! Death could not hold Him or defeat Him! David knew this!

This very thought releases more energy and strength to fight and win! In 1 Chronicles 5, we see that it only took a little over 5,000 men to overtake, kill and capture over a hundred thousand! The Lord of hosts was with them and the Lord of Host is with us today!

He is the same God, yesterday, today and forever! I already see the end…we win with great victory!

If satan had not seen where we were going, he would have no need to bring out all his so called "big guns!" He who fights against our God, as Goliath learned, is the fool who dies and falls by the wayside while we carry away all the spoils! Our captain is the Lord of Hosts! When we go forth in His name, enemies have to fall, all have to surrender.

It makes no difference to God if we be a small number

or a great number! One—God—is the army! Even if we be few we win, no matter the size of the enemy! Our confidence need only be in our Lord alone! He is our sword, our shield, with power to deflect every move of the enemy. He will too!

Our report will always be, "WE WON," for the battle belongs to our great and mighty God!

Do not shrink back when it looks like you are outnumbered and the enemy "appears to be winning!" Do not shrink back when you get into the "impossible place", the hard difficulties! Do not even flinch at wounds, pain, or even death. Keep wielding His sword with all your might! Wound with the sword until the slain enemies lie around you in heaps! The battle is our Lord's and He will deliver every enemy into our hands!

We will be the one who cuts the enemy's head off. We will be the one who decides if we want to carry his head, (his dead thinking), around to show our trophy of battle!

Our footing is sure, our hands and fingers are strong in battle. Our zeal is like the flame of a roaring hot fire, our roar is the roar of a lion! With this we, without shame or fear, RUN into the enemies camp! The enemy will fly then like chaff in a hurricane wind!

We are undefeated! We win, we rule, today and forever with our Captain the Lord of Hosts! *Then David said to the Philistine, you come to me with a sword, spear, and javelin. I come to you in the name of the Lord of Hosts, the God of the armies of Israel, whom you have defied.... I will give the carcasses of the hosts of the Philistines this day unto the birds of the air and the wild beast of the earth, that all the earth may know that there is a God in Israel!"* 1 Sam 17:45,46.

He did it then! He will do it again! JUST FOR YOU!!!

AUTHORITY

*You have made him to have dominion
over the works of your hands;
You have put ALL things under his feet!*
Psalm 8:6

That's ALL things! All things even includes time! Our ability to exercise authority over all the earth is dependent on our willingness to submit, to serve, and obey the living God who holds authority over us.

No one or anything has authority over us unless we grant it! This includes speaking things into your life. No one can tell you how far you can go, what you can do, what you can be, what you can own or what you can say!

Faith knows this! You do not have to bow to the things of the world. The world does not dictate your life. If Jesus is Lord of your life, you are not of this world, but a citizen of the Kingdom of God. Faith in your King, your Lord dictates what you can and will receive.

It's NOW faith! *NOW FAITH, is the substance of things hoped for, the evidence of things not seen*, Hebrews 11:1. No doctor can tell you how much time you have to live.

When Adam and Eve fell into sin we lost our eternal nature. We were designed to be forever, for eternity. When we were cut off from eternity, time began, and we started living in time in this world. Time then started dictating to us.

Jesus always brought eternity into time with His immediatelies and suddenlies! God tells us in His word when we pray. believe that we receive it and it is ours. It will become tangible! We receive what we believed for that day, what we asked God for, or what we asked Him to do!

We have authority over ALL things!!! We can live an undefeated life of faith!

Take authority over that disease, that situation, sickness, the mountain, the flood, the hurricane or a storm!!! You have authority, use it!!! That authority is in the name of Jesus Christ of Nazareth!!! Walk undefeated today, never giving up your God given authority!

ALL things are under your feet!

TODAY!!!

RESPECT

We respect what we believe in!

If I respect you, I show consideration for your feelings, even though they may differ from mine. Wisdom honors that person or thing that is respected. I can respect your feelings, your property and or your position! I can plan with respect for the future.

If you are a person who is respectful then I know you learned it, embraced it.

If you are a person who is respected, then you earned it.

If you are thoughtful, if you care about other's feelings, you will respect them. Respect for another is simply a choice.

Many who have been respected, upon making a mistake, have lost the respect others had for them. Respect is a tremendous part of honoring. A boss, a person, a leader, even a mate can lose another's respect. In silence, respect takes its leave.

Loss of respect is sometimes a great loss. Loosing respect is not always because of deeds but also by wrong words. Who and what I respect is a definite measurement of my greatness—my greatness in the eyes of God and others!

Respect without honor is a lack. If I do not respect you I cannot honestly honor you. A person disrespected loses their desire to perform or produce. Jesus did! At one time, Jesus did no mighty works because of a lack of respect for miracle **power** not honored. The word does not say He could not. No, it was not because He could not. Matthew 13:57,58 tells us: *…A prophet is not without honor, save in his own country, in his own house. And He did not many mighty works there because of their unbelief.* No appreciation, no respect, no honor found there! He lost all desire to perform.

Appreciation, respect, and honor feed the desire in our natural man to do well! Be a person of real honor, real character, respect differences!

It means you made a choice for greatness!

ANXIETY

When we allow feelings of worry and trouble,
caused by fear,
we experience anxiety.

Fear is believing in evil. Fear of loss can become what the world now labels as "anxiety attacks." When we let fear take hold this is what happens in our minds and hearts. This can even lead to panic. Anxiety is simply a lack of trust in God. There is a difference between faith and trust!

The baby jumping on the **bed** knows his father loves him, he has faith in him. When the father tells the child to, "Jump and I'll catch you," this will require more than faith! It will require trust that his father will do what he said.

No matter what circumstances we face, we must believe in the awesome love and care our Heavenly Father has for us! If we really believe Him and what He says we can trust more easily. The Israelites did not really believe God loved them. He continued loving them even when they did not believe it.

He loves us today, and when HE says, "Jump out with your faith, and I will catch you," He will do it! His ability to be trusted is in every act Jesus did! One of my earliest mentors, Kenneth Hagan Sr., said that it took him three months to receive and apply the following scriptures. Matthew 6:25-34:

> 25 Therefore I say unto you, Take no thought for your life, what ye shall eat, or what ye shall drink; nor yet for your body, what ye shall put on. Is not the life more than meat, and the body than raiment?
> 26 Behold the fowls of the air: for they sow not, neither do they reap, nor gather into barns; yet your heavenly Father feedeth them. Are ye not much better than they?
> 27 Which of you by taking thought can add one cubit unto his stature?
> 28 And why take ye thought for raiment? Consider the lilies of the field, how they grow; they toil not, neither do they spin:
> 29 And yet I say unto you, That even Solomon in all his glory was not arrayed like one of these.
> 30 Wherefore, if God so clothe the grass of the field, which today is, and tomorrow is cast into the oven, [shall He] not much more [clothe] you, O ye of little faith?
> 31 Therefore take no thought, saying, What shall we eat? or, What shall we drink? or, Wherewithal shall we be clothed?
> 32 (For after all these things do the Gentiles seek:) for your heavenly Father knoweth that ye have need of all these things.
> 33 But seek ye first the kingdom of God, and His righteousness; and all these things shall be added unto you.
> 34 Take therefore no thought for the morrow: for the morrow shall take thought for the things of itself. Sufficient unto the day [is] the evil thereof.

Read that until you receive it!

Jesus is asking, "Why are you not trusting me to be there for you?" *Therefore do not worry about tomorrow, for tomorrow will worry about its own thing. Sufficient for the day is its own troubles*—Matthew 6:34.

Don't lean to your own understanding of things happening around you! Trust in our Heavenly Father...there is no place to trust that is any greater or purer! Go ahead and jump. If He has asked you to jump, He is going to catch you in His loving arms! Not only that but His heart will become merry from your trust in him!!!

Do it today!!!

PROTOCOL

Protocol...one of my favorite subjects!

Protocol is simply and most always a written or unwritten rule of behavior, enforced or not. It's the rule for excellence in proper behavior, and always births good will.

Queen Victoria's reign has been aptly described as the reign of protocol! Protocol involves interacting, communicating, and honor. There are many aspects of protocol. There is the protocol of international politics, diplomacy, and for affairs of state. Showing proper respect in appropriate places and in proper ways to leaders is proper protocol.

Protocol, like music, crosses boundaries of nations, going international. There is a business protocol, seating, addressing, and order, even attire is involved in proper protocol. Protocol can be as simple as acknowledgement of the standing of those around you. 49% of employers and colleges surveyed in 2005 stated that non-traditional attire would be a strong influence in their opinion for a potential applicant. We see that protocol in attire carries heavy weight.

Protocol is always based in the principles of our love

for God, reverence for Him, respect, civility, and our character. There are no limits to the heights of excellence in protocol. It is behavior, and it is either right or wrong, varying from society to society.

An uneducated man, but one who loves Jesus, will be able to navigate with the Holy Spirit in proper protocol anywhere, at any time, with anyone. He just needs to know the guide line: *Let nothing be done through selfish ambition or conceit, but in lowliness of mind let each esteem others better than himself.*—Philippians 2:3.

I challenge you to excellence in protocol today in all your behavior! It can start today and become a mark of your character forever!!!

Proper protocol can lead to advancement
and
excellence in character.

FEELINGS

"Feelings,"…as my mentor,
Dr. Mike Murdock says,
"are not you."

A feeling is an emotion, and it can change in a moment's notice. It can simply be an impression. It can also be an illusion.

A feeling can be just being conscience of something or someone. Many have become deceived because they thought their feeling was a fact.

We can liken feelings to boxcars on a train. Life is like a train traveling through different places, through different lives. Feelings cannot and will not pull that train. Feelings are like the different names on boxcars! Those boxcars are pulled by the engine, the engine we will call truth.

It is the truth that takes us through life. We cannot altar the truth.

Feelings can be altered in seconds. Feelings can vary from day to day from circumstances, words, actions of others, etc. A tragedy is the decision based on no fact but all feelings. Those kind of decisions create shaking foundations that will cause what is built upon them to collapse. That is a sand foundation.

- Is it a feeling or fact?
- What has God said.
- Is there scripture to back it up?
- Has God confirmed from the mouth of two or three witnesses?
- What did the wisdom found in a multitude of counselors reveal?

We do not have to make mistakes based on feelings! Our train of life must be pulled by the engine of truth, the real facts. *And every one that heareth these sayings of mine, and doeth them not, shall be likened unto a foolish man, which built his house upon the sand*—Matthew 7:26.

Anything built outside of truth will never stand the very first storm. This is what Jesus wanted us to know!!! It is good news for knowing how to build and what to build on! He loved us so much He taught us how to be successful by obedience to truth, not our feelings.

Great news today!!!
Still!!!

PROCESS

Oh, such a tough word,
such a tough thing!

Nobody likes "the process!" However, there is no purpose without process. In order to have forward movement, there must be process! Everything we see, everything we encounter has become because of a process.

The process is not an easy journey for most all things to come forward or for us to progress, to become. When we are saved, we do not suddenly become a perfected human being. We learn, we grow, then we grow, and then we know.

To become like Christ is a process, to become a good person with honor and greatness is a process. The speed of much of the process is determined by our attitude and our desire for change, as well as what we are exposed to. If we are not making progress, we are merely standing still and not moving forward in that goal, in that purpose.

God uses trials of faith, of fire, and of trust in the process of building character in us. There are books, mentors, experiences that help us through the process, even when the book, the mentor, or the experience seems to be harsh.

Change happens in the process of becoming and it is a very hard thing sometimes. It is hard to hear, hard to do, and at times, very painful. It is through these times of learning that we began to arrive at our purpose.

Everything you buy, everything you eat had to begin with a process to become. Your seed goes through a process before it can become your harvest. Godly relationships are a process to develop great purpose.

God had a purpose in sending His Son, but He went through a process. Salvation is a process, beginning with believing Jesus Christ is Savior:

Whom shall he teach knowledge, and whom shall he make to understand doctrine? Them that are weaned from the milk and drawn from the breast. For precept must be upon precept, precept upon precept; line upon line; here a little, and there a little—Isaiah 28:9-10.

You are unlimited to what you can learn,
what you can become.
The only requirement is
obedience to God
and
the desire for your purpose!!!

INTERESTS

Satan's trap for sure!!!
Ever really given thought to your interests?
What you care about;
what you want to know more about?

Much could be said about interests. We will dwell here mostly on the things that affect our spiritual life. An interest is anything that arouses feelings of wanting to know, wanting to have.

Your interests, before you got saved were those generated by a mind of flesh. When God saves your soul, He does not save your mind. Through study and much learning you become more interested in the things of God.

The things of God are the lasting things, the real things creating interests without end! God can hold the smartest man's interest now and on through eternity.

Most of us are easily swayed back into sin when we first start our walk with God! "Why is this?" you say. It's because we still have interests in our lives that are not of God. We must read His word and learn from those God places in our lives to change this, to achieve the mind of

Christ. Any of those interests that we have not overcome will one day overcome us. This is satan's trapdoor into our mind.

Our interests can be our weaknesses, something that we indulged in, habits before giving our lives over to Christ. I promise you, satan knows your weaknesses better than you do and he will use that to get a stronghold in your mind, life, and words.

When satan wants to derail you, he will always start a relationship with something that interests you. When satan wants to befriend you, he does not try to do it by talking about or introducing that which is of no interest to you. He will create a common bond, a common interest, so he can start building a "friendship." Do I need to say how many satan has lured into his camp just because one showed interest in whatever bait he used? The bait was your interests, and he pulled you right in.

Do you know your own interests? Do you know which of your interests could be of worldly things; in Godly things? Satan does not have much of a chance when our interests are only God centered.

Do you know the purposes of your different friendships? It is important to know. *And do not be CONFORMED to this world, but be ye transformed by the renewing of your mind, that you may prove what is that good and ACCEPTABLE and perfect will of God*, Romans12:2.

Look at your interests. They may reveal the reason for past mistakes as well as make for fewer mistakes in your future!

Awesome thought… brighter tomorrows!!!
Measure and weigh your interests
to those of God for you now!!!

CREDIBILITY

How others see you.

Credibility, one of the top priorities for your life along with trustworthiness and your souls salvation!

Credibility is the most important possession you have or will ever own. When your credibility is gone, there is nothing else left to be said. It is a long, long, and hard road back once credibility is lost.

I have never been sure, except for God and His miracles, that a person could ever restore their own credibility. For one to learn credibility he must first learn what truth is, and how important truth is.

Credibility is truth in the most inward parts. For the person with true credibility, the worst insult you could ever pay him is to doubt or question his credibility. That carries great, great pain with it and righteous anger as well. People have allowed satan to use them many times to attempt to destroy a great person's credibility. Many, many times this has happened!

The real truth is this: no one can really destroy your

credibility except you, yourself. Someone has said many years ago, "To thine own self be true." When a credible person is tempted to do or say something that is not truth, goodness, and right, whether anyone else be present, they will honor themselves by never indulging. This not only keeps their credibility honorable, but God is also honored as well as His Word.

NO deceit was found in the mouth of Jesus!
NONE!!!

We want to be like Jesus, but without credibility it is impossible! God and holiness demands honesty in the most innermost parts of our hearts, of our lives. This is the pure heart! Blessed are those with a pure heart for they shall see God!!!

A person who is credible is one who will like himself. He is healthy mentally and spiritually. To look you in the eye with direct honesty is no problem for him! *A good name is rather to be chosen than great riches, and loving favour rather than silver and gold*—Proverbs 22:1.

God's opinion and love of credibility is so great He gave us that measurement so we could see how important it is!!! Much, much more important than money or anything it will ever buy!

Protect yourself!
Protect your credibility today by thinking and acting in righteous living in all aspects of your life!!!
Be an open book!
You can!!!
Credibility is at the top of my list for myself,
for others.
It should be your priority as well!

TITHES

Tithing is the gateway
of blessings into your life.

Tithing is the first proof that you honor God for what He has given you. He gave you health and intelligence to do a work. You are simply recognizing this. It is your proof that you honor Him.

You think of yourself as a good person and good people want more people to be good and more good things to happen—right? This is your opportunity!

Tithes are used for good things, for the expansion of good things and not evil. Many, many good things are done with tithes. If I were the friend who gave you your home, car, job, family and children, making it possible for you to live in blessings, would you think of me? Would you, even not knowing the principles of God, want to do something to give back to me....something?

This is what God does each and every day. Our tithes are our insurance premium that covers the rest of our money and also all the others things we own and/or don't yet own! God's only challenge to you in the entire Word of

God is to obey Him, the King, and He will rebuke the devourer for your sake. This is the greatest security you have; the best insurance you will ever own for covering your things! Ever!!!

You pay taxes to the government, but the government does not give you security. God gives you security and here is where you find it! He only asks for 10%, yet He gives you much more than that to keep! He is an amazing and loving King! He longs to bless you, to give you more!

Try it, like He said, and see!!! *Bring ye all the tithes into the storehouse, that there may be meat in Mine house and prove Me now herewith, saith the Lord of hosts, if I will not open you the windows of heaven, and pour you out a blessing that there shall not be room enough to receive it!* Malachi 3:10.

I challenge you to try it! Quote God's word to Him and do this for one year and see what happens to your life!!! I promise, you will be amazed at the blessings of God to you!!!

Don't rob God of the opportunity to bless your life!!!
Start tithing today!!!

HONOR

What is honor—really?

True honor is something that is a rare blessing, coveted by many; however, not everyone will receive this great blessing! It is not just dependent upon a person seeing the need for honor, but it also depends on other things, even your geological location.

Jesus did not do miracles in a place where there was no honor for Him as the Son of God, or for His assignment. The seed for honor is humility. The person who quickly recognizes who to honor; what to honor, will always be a person who has been dishonored the most.

The greater the show of honor from an individual, the greater the seed of humility that has been sown.

God tells men, "honor your wives." Men who are not honored by their wives lose their capacity to be all they can be! If there is no honor shown to the proper person, creativity and happiness will soon cease to exit.

Much honor is learned by observation. Proper protocol demands proper honor. Proper application of honor is sometimes caught by observations of it being exhibited. (Children to parents, the flag, mother to dad, etc.)

One can show honor in many ways, however it is not true honor if it is not from the heart and for godly standards. No one honors nor plans honor for himself, that is not honor. I like to say that honor is a culture, overriding backgrounds and races. I like to describe it as a culture of the heart. It is from the heart that all things given will flow toward us, things in deeds and words.

No one is a better recipient of honor than the one with experiences of dishonor. God frowns upon the lack of it. He said leave that place, shake anything off you which attached itself to you in that place and don't look back.

Do not expect honor where you did not sow it in love and humility. Honor carries in its hand an instant harvest. Humility with proper protocol can release the harvest of honor into your life. Honor is something we do—an action—HONOR.

"Honor must become your seed before it becomes your harvest" (Dr. Mike Murdock). I believe he said in one sentence what I explained in a paragraph! I honor his depth of thought here; his brilliance. *By humility and the fear of the Lord are riches and honor and life*—Proverbs 27:4.

So you see, everyone can be a receiver of honor. It is up to you. Give it today and you shall receive it in your tomorrows!!!

God said so!!!

SALVATION

The saving of something.... is salvation.

In Christianity we know that salvation is the saving of our soul—forever, from death and from hell. Jesus came to save us from hell, not to send us to hell. He loved what He created.

Man is a creation of God, and given a free will. God quickly came to the rescue when He saw that we would be tempted as mere humans and miss the mark of holiness. He loved us so much He could not bear the thought of losing us from Himself forever for He is Holy. He gave us the plan of salvation to insure the fact if we wanted a savior, we could have one. So, He sent his son Jesus.

I like to think of what my mentor, Dr. Murdock, says is the reasons why we should recognize we need a savior. We need forgiveness, to be cleansed from our sins. We have all done wrong. We need a friend that will never leave us, never forsake us, who loves us, and is a whole lot smarter than we are, to be a real friend.

Thirdly, we need a future. You see, without a savior, we have no future when we die. We are lost to satan and hell forever. We need Jesus.

If there were no heaven, no hell, I would still live as a Christian because it is the very best there is in this world to choose from. The good news is there is a heaven. Those who make Jesus their salvation and obey him as King will one day live there forever!!!

Isn't that a beautiful picture of love rescuing and rewarding? We can be assured of our salvation for our soul by receiving Jesus as Savior. Not only that but we can have protection and multiplication for our possessions on this earth by giving to Him the tithe, right off the top. We now have salvation for our souls forever and protection and increase for our stuff on this earth by honoring Him as King with our tithes.

What more could we ask for in a plan of salvation for us? What more love could anyone ever give us than to die for us on a cross so we could have all that? He is our bridge of salvation from this world into eternal life!

For God so loved the world that he gave his only begotten son that WHOSOEVER believes on him shall be saved—John 3:16.

You can know NOW that you are going to heaven if you die today. All of this is because of God's great love for you!

He is a good God!!!

TRIUMPH

Oh yes, if it has been a battle there will be a victory. Keep fighting until you win!!!

If there has been a victory there should be a celebration in triumph! Jesus triumphant entry into Jerusalem was celebration of His Messiahship proclaimed in Zechariah 9:9.

When there is triumph people are moved as they were that day! Jesus was also riding in triumph over sin and satan for He was both man and God! Our King of Kings and Lord of Lords road into Jerusalem as Victor!

When God raises you up, there is victory, there is triumph! Triumph is the celebrating of our victory! When God does this it is celebration and triumph that is sweet, for God is the one who raises you up! Triumph is the celebrating and the honoring of one who is worthy.

Ball teams have triumphant entries back into their home towns after great victories! Sinners receive triumphant entry INTO The Kingdom when they are born again! Triumph over the old life, sin, and satan!

In ancient Rome there was ceremonial entrance of a victorious commander with his army, spoils of war, and his captives. In this way he was honored by the Roman Senate. This was his celebrated moment of triumph for important military or naval battles.

Imagine coming into the presence of God, to the throne of God, with our victories in our hand, and a crown to lay before Jesus, and our spoils covering us! (Our anointing from these battles are our spoils.)

We honor great people, great leaders with ceremonies and celebrations of the battle won, and victory gained in overcoming! Expect great entrance into that which God has promised you! It will happen, He said it and He will do it! Those who love you will help you celebrate in your triumph! Imagine entrance into heaven as an overcomer to receive the crowns as heaven celebrates you!

Hosanna to the Son of David! ...Blessed is he who comes in the name of the Lord! Hosanna in the highest!!!—Matthew 21:9.

Get ready for your celebration. Get ready for your triumphant entry into the place God designed only for you! Those who expect, those who have faith will receive God's promise for their life!

Expect today!!! Our God is a rewarder!!!
Receive with NOW faith your reward and triumph!!!
TODAY!!!

SORROW

When sorrow came, what was going on in your life?
Evil causes sorrow.
God does not have it in his hand to give anyone.
Love does not create sorrow.
God is love.

You may ask then why do we have to experience sorrow in our lives? Much of the time it is not of our own doing. Of course there is death, it is appointed unto every man to one day die or be taken by our King as were Enoch and Elijah. As long as man can make a decision there will be, somewhere, the consequence of that decision.

Good decisions will reap great and good consequences. Bad and evil decisions will always reap the consequences of sorrow and pain for that person and those associated with his or her life. People will always make mistakes as long as they remain human. Sometimes these are not sins, just mistakes, but sometimes reaping tragic results.

The more we consult with the Holy Spirit, the closer we walk to the Him seeking direction for our lives, the less sorrow we will encounter. We get caught in the backwash of other's sins and decisions many times that will cause us great sorrow. The people who are closest to us, those to whom we have granted access are the ones that will be responsible for much of our pain.

The word of God tells us to guard our affections, guard our heart. This is the reason God told us that. Guarding the access we give those around us will eliminate a lot of sorrow and pain. We must let Holy Spirit guide us in relationships with the discernment He gives to us. Man is free to make decisions and many of those will not be godly decisions. Those are the ones that bring pain and sorrow. Every wrong decision we make will affect many, many lives!

Don't waste your sorrow, take full advantage of it. It will birth understandings and truths in your life like nothing else can. Pain births much knowledge and understanding. When it comes time to love your brother with an understanding ministry for his pain, you will be able to speak from experience. Do not ever tell any person that they should not feel this way. There is much to be learned during a season of sorrow, and a lot more revelation of God can be received. This is why I say, don't waste that sorrow!!!

> *We know that all things work together for good to them that love God, to them who are the called according to His purpose*—Romans 8:28!

> If you love God, He has made you this promise! NEVER forget it!!!

PEACE PART 1

"Peace is not the absence of conflict…
it is the absence of inner conflict."

Those are words of my mentor, Dr. Mike Murdock. A sure clue for knowing a person has not come to peace of mind is the man who is consistently talking. This man has no peace. When Jesus comes to live in your life peace will come. He is the Prince of Peace. He becomes your peace.

When you start doing things the right way and honoring God's instructions and laws in your life you began to live in peace. Peace is one of His gifts for you. When your mind is filled with God's Word and His promises, great peace stills the mind.

Not everyone will reach this great resting place of peace, for they never learn that it is very safe and secure to trust our Prince of Peace. Many times peace is referred to as a river, for it flows like a quiet though always moving river flowing into and from your being.

When in doubt about a direction or a decision, the word of God says to follow the path of peace for it is always where our King is. The closer you walk to God, the greater your peace. The spirit of peace can even be a presence that can be felt exuding from your very presence when you are filled with peace from heaven. Peace came to earth when Jesus came into this world:

> *And the peace of God, which passeth all understanding, shall keep your hearts and minds through Christ Jesus*—Philippians 4:7.

You can have the most perfect peace possible in this world today!

Receive Jesus—receive peace today!

PLANS

How are your plans working out for you?
Are you working your plan or is it working you?

In order to achieve our dream we must have a plan. The plan is the foundation for goals and dreams. We must also know our weaknesses for those weaknesses are what satan will use to hinder our plan that will take us to our dream. When he wants to do this he will bring a plan loaded with enticements for our weaknesses in order to stop the plan to achieve that dream and to please God.

This is the counterfeit. The bigger the plan God has for you, the stronger and more often satan will come against it with a substitute. The substitute could even look good! Recognize this and know that everything and everybody connected to a counterfeit do not belong in your life.

No matter how involved or attached you may become, counterfeits must be completely torn from your heart and your life. Give it to God. Let Him decide what He will do with it, if anything at all!

If you fall for the substitute you will not stop the plan of

God, you may cause it to be delayed and you will most certainly pay the price for wrong choices, and so will others. When we realize we have fallen for the counterfeit it is very painful to let go, but must it be torn from the heart until every piece is history. If you buy into the counterfeit then you will have to eliminate it from your life and everything and everyone that came with it in order for you to see God's great and real plan for you.

God is a jealous God and He will share with no one His plan for you or your life. Understand this! If you don't give the counterfeit up, God will take it from you Himself. The plan God has for our lives is only revealed in part—in pieces! Satan's plan will be showing all its enticements at once. We must make our plans with God or satan will be who and what is happening while we are making <u>our</u> plans.

God's plan is the one that will take faith. It always requires faith to recognize and embrace for it is always bigger than ourselves. Today the plans of God are more significant than ever for they are designed to bring His coming.

You don't really think God will change his mind for you, do you? You may have to do some things to make His plan work that you did not plan on doing. You may have to say some things you did not plan on saying—this is God at work. Only His plan will work in your life to usher in the dream.

We are to make the plans to achieve our goals and dreams, but we cannot do it without God in it.

Have you talked to God about His plan or do you constantly talk with God about your plan?

Who and what is effected by your plans? Do they know?

A plan simply remains "only a plan" if there is no

commitment. Unsecured plans are plans that stand to remain a great loss to you and others. There must be the securing of those things that will fulfill God's plan for you. You can plan and set goals, but you must allow God to order your steps. When He starts ordering your steps, simply submit to His will and what He wants and how He wants to do it. He has seen your life from the beginning and He already knows His plan to bring you to a good end.

He gave Holy Spirit to you to help you through your decisions Consult Him often! God has supplied you with help...have you recognized the help God has sent you? It is probably not your family, it may be someone of the same gender, it is probably going to be your very best friend. It can be your helpmate.

God is serious and has serious plans, but He will not always deal gently with slack, for He is not slack concerning His promises to His children. One decision sets the plan of God in place; commitment will keep it there.

David said when I put my trust in those who cannot help, my plans perish. In Proverbs 16:9 we find, *A man's heart plans his way, but the Lord directs his steps.* Make your decision today to allow God the room He wants in your plans! Then let Him grow those plans—enlarging you along with them. Changing your plan to agree with the purposes of God and His plan is the seed for excellence in obedience! Do it today!!!

Delayed obedience is disobedience! You have finally arrived at your moment of faith, take the leap with trust in an Almighty God for He will be there for you without fail!!!

Change chaos into wisdom and the uncertain into security!!
Today!!!
You are only one decision away........Don't make another mistake!!!
Do it today!!!

HARVEST

Have you checked your harvest lately?

Our seeds, decisions and words are the three things that bring our harvest. Our harvest is whatever the yield is, the result or consequences of those three things.

A farmer plants seeds at the right time to produce the plants that will bring a harvest of fruits or vegetables. We plant seeds each day we live that determine what our harvest will be and the size of it.

Our seeds are what we give to one another, to the ministry that is doing a good work, even what we give to our enemy. Our gifts, offerings, our help to the poor are all seeds. When we give anything, our time, our talents, our love, understanding, mercy—we are sowing seeds!

It does not matter what we give whether it be from our spiritual life, emotional life, physical life, even from our personality, it becomes a seed sown. We make decisions that bring results to us. These are either godly decisions or they are worldly decisions. Depending on which one, that will be what determines the season and that will be the harvest of that decision.

If we pray, wait for God to answer, and walk in the path of peace then we know the decision will bring a good harvest. If we rush—go without any counseling, without the proper knowledge, and without weighing the consequences—then we will reap a very unsatisfactory harvest.

Then, there are the seeds of our words. We speak blessings which are faith words, good words every single day. They are either words of truth, fitting words, comforting words, words of hope, of life, of inspiration, and encouragement, or they are not.

Words that damage another, hurt the heart of another, and unkind words that destroy and bring grief are not words of life and blessings. We should inventory our vocabulary and see what kind of words we are using. If we speak these words that release bad seeds into others, then that is the seed that we have sown that brings us a painful harvest.

The world has a saying that, "What goes around comes around." That is true but it is simply a takeoff of what the word of God says. Here is what the word of God says. He promised us a harvest but we get to choose which one we prefer by these three ways we choose to sow seeds.

Do not be deceived, God is not mocked; for whatsoever a man sows, that he will also reap— Galatians 6:5.

God is a good God. He gave us the whole world and then gave us a choice of what we could reap from it in our lifetime and after death. It is a generational seed we sow each day so think seriously about it for it is your life now and in the judgment day.

God is a good God!!!
He is so good!!!

Think!!!

ETHICS

"Oh!" you may say.
"Now you are getting real serious for sure!"

Yes, I am. Ethics are a very serious thing and something that should be taught. Ethics is simply the study of right and wrong. We have so many people today who are lacking in many areas of good ethics! I believe the more godly a person is the greater their ethics in everyday life, no matter what area it is in.

If you have good work habits and performance you are considered someone with good work ethics. This is something to be desired, but it is not something that everyone participates in. I say, "participates in," because cultivating good ethics in any arena is a choice and can become another description of us personally.

A list of different areas where we find a display of ethics would include work, study, morality, duty, and/or judgment. They can be formal or professional rules of conduct, of behavior. Ethics are merely rules of right or wrong. People can view all areas of our life and if they give us much thought they can say whether we have great work ethics or moral ethics or whatever area it is that is being witnessed or discussed.

A person of excellence will be found to have good ethics in all areas of their life. They will not stoop to wrong, it is below their dignity, their rules for conduct, and below their standards of excellence.

Sometimes when hiring an employee, the ex-employer may be asked this question: "What kind of work ethics does this person have?" When voting for someone for an office it may be asked: "What kind of moral ethics does this person have?"

A man who has an employee with good work ethics, is a blessed man. So is the man who has a leader with good moral ethics!

Good ethics in all areas is something to work for, something to achieve and something to be both greatly desired and admired! If we are working to please the Lord in all areas of our life, then we will not have to worry about our ethics because the Word of God teaches this, though many times this particular study of ethics may not be taught.

Do you know the right way to do things? There is a right way and a wrong way to do things!!! Seek, ask, knock, read until you find the right way to do it!

Whatever your hand finds to do, do it with your might; for thee is no work or device or knowledge or wisdom in the grave where you are going, Ecclesiastes 9:10.

If we do all things as unto the Lord, then we will not be ashamed of our ethics—today or ever!

Let's remember that! O.k.?

ATTITUDE

What attitude does your face—your eyes portray?

Everybody talks about a person's attitude when it is really bad, really good, or when they are impressed! What is your outlook towards different people, people in general, circumstances or things touching your life?

Your attitude is not just words. Your attitude can be displayed by your actions, body language, reactions, emotions, even your posture! There is something about an attitude that is very memorable, especially when it is unusual. People judge us by our attitude in these different areas.

A good rule of thumb for developing a good attitude is remembering that there is something good in every single thing and every single human being! Then the second step is to be grateful for that fact!!! After all, it could have been all bad.

Negative feelings that are harbored are the seeds for bad attitudes. Selfishness is another seed for a bad attitude. When I say bad attitude, I am saying it is a negative attitude producing no joy, no happiness within the person or the victim of the attitude.

If you look at things in a positive way and recognize the good in everyday life you will become a person with a good attitude. When you see the results of the good attitude and what it is bringing to you then you will become even more interested in developing an even greater attitude.

A person in bad circumstances, but with a great attitude about life, is someone to be admired, giving us something to be desired! A person who has a good attitude will have no problems looking at things with a positive attitude and creating faith and happiness in others. People with great attitudes are people who inspire us to be better, do better, think better, think higher.

I guess what I am trying to say is that great attitudes are like a great puff of wind that carries all the debris away and leaves us feeling refreshed and ready to tackle anything. We begin to think, "If they can have that kind of attitude, so can I!!!" Great attitudes are contagious!

The person with a bad attitude is the person who is thinking of themselves.

The person with the great attitude is bored thinking of himself! He is always thinking of others and all the good in others and all the good in the happenings around them!!! He doesn't entertain the negative and he does not exude negative, but life and faith!!!

Do you have an attitude that people admire or do you complain and moan about every little thing? I have heard it said that your attitude determines your altitude. I say your attitude determines your favor with God and man!!!

Finally, brethren, whatsoever things are true, whatsoever things are noble, whatsoever things are just, whatsoever things are pure, whatsoever things are of good report, if there is any virtue and if there is anything praise worthy, mediate on these things—Philippians 4:81!

If we do this, there will be no need for a bad attitude. Then people will say, "*I thank my God in all my remembrance of you*!"

Wouldn't that be a great reputation to have about our attitude?

Yes!!!

REFLECTION

You may ask, "What is the value of reflection?"

When we are in reflection, we are doing some really careful thinking! I like to reflect upon things, people, conversations, and words that were spoken; maybe some things I saw. I like to each day spend a little time scanning yesterday in my mind. I ask myself many questions. Questions I might ask myself are some of these:

- What could I have done differently?
- What could I have done better?
- What do I see in my yesterday that I need to eliminate from my present and my future?
- What did that person really mean?
- What was my response to each one?
- Did I do all I could have done in every circumstance I was in yesterday?
- Did I see and take advantage of all the opportunities that God gave to me?

I am not speaking here of delving into your past history! I am talking about just recently, maybe the day before...

- What did I learn?
- How was it taught to me—was it in a word, a deed?
- Do I need to learn from a mistake I saw someone make yesterday?
- What do I need to pray for?

I carefully reflect on all the things and people who are touching my life with words and deeds.

- Is God pleased with what I did yesterday?
- Is He pleased with how I handled things yesterday?
- Is He pleased with what I said yesterday?

The Holy Spirit is always with me as I ask Him to search my life, search my heart, for I am willing to walk with Him as he shows me what I need to change—what I need to ask forgiveness for!

We must reflect…let the Holy Spirit search our lives, our thoughts, our deeds and our words then welcome His purification so we can come into God's presence.

An example of reflection is the Bronze Laver in the tabernacle. Here we can see the reflection of ourselves in the water and after looking at ourselves in all honesty, we then allow the water, symbolic of the Holy Spirit, to wash our hands so we can come into the Presence of God.

We reflect on what we have seen in God's word.

Then of course there is the reflection on God's creation, His majesty; His awesome work in our lives and in the world.

There is more to reflect upon than there is space and time to talk or write about! We lose an opportunity to see great beauty when we don't take the time to reflect. David was a man of reflection. I am sure he must have developed this habit when he was alone on the countryside sleeping under the stars reflecting on what God had taught him. There he learned about his own Great Shepherd as he tended the sheep and saw His glory in the heavens. David said, *The Lord is high above all nations, His glory above the heavens! Who is like the Lord our God, who dwells on high?*—Psalm 113:4,5. In his reflection of God and His creation, praise was born in David's heart and mind, flooding his mouth with song!

Reflection is a good thing. Reflection requires time, but what you will see will be well worth it…

Think about it…..

ANGER

What is anger?
Isn't it a sin?
How can anger be avoided?

Everybody is capable of anger. Everyone is going to experience anger at some point in time—perhaps many times in one's life. It is not a sin to become angry. Anger is a healthy emotion. What makes it unhealthy is how we act or react in anger.

The word of God is very clear about this. God wanted us to know it is okay to be angry...

> *Be ye angry, and sin not; let not the sun go down upon our wrath; ...Let all bitterness, and wrath, and anger, clamour, and evil speaking, be put away from you with malice....: And be ye kind one to another, tenderhearted, forgiving one another even as God for Christ's sake hath forgiven you,* Ephesians 4:26, 31, 32.

When we say the wrong things in anger—we sin. We hurt and injure—sometimes for a lifetime—with words spoken in anger. If you cannot control your words or your actions in an angry moment, simply walk away and take time to think about it, how to handle it and what you need to do.

Anger is energy. To get angry about the right things is a good thing. That is righteous anger. We must focus anger properly—whether it is right or wrong—with the right solution. Anger—pent up—becomes bitterness and resentment that can become a very bitter and destructive pool of words or actions.

We must first remember that the real reason we are angry is because someone did not do it our way, or something did not go our way. Self-centered people are the people who are most easily aroused to anger. This is because things don't suit them and this angers them. This person must learn to relax. Sometimes these are the ones who are driven by success or they cannot deal very well with incompetence.

Anger must be dealt with by talking with someone—preferably, the person to whom one is reacting in an angry fashion. Forgiveness has to happen for peace to reign again. Sometimes it helps if we remember the mistakes we have made and that everyone is to be respected even when wrong if for no other reason—because they are made in the image of our God.

Talk to God about it, tell Him how you feel, He will hear, He will help you understand the reasoning behind your anger. You will feel better. A simple prayer will cause you to take the right action, speak the right words and to be able to forgive again.

Choose soft words! The Word of God says, *a soft answer turns away wrath, but a grievous word will stir up anger.* As you grow in the Lord, you will still experience anger, but it will become easier for you to deal with it in a more mature way.

"Anger is simply passion requiring an appropriate focus!"—words of my mentor, Dr. Mike Murdock. Appropriate words of wisdom from my wisdom teacher! Think about that and find the appropriate focus, the appropriate time, the appropriate words and actions as you release your anger.

Forgive all and live a pure life before our God!
You can do this!

FREEDOM

Do you understand the responsibility and cost of freedom? Do you know its value?

Freedom is the most sought after thing in the world, but it is the most abused thing on the earth! It is one of the two things that are always taken for granted until you think you are losing them; the other one is health.

Living without any controls on us, having the liberty to do and say as we desire and having all the power to carry out those desires is a place of great happiness and creativeness!

The down side of that is the fact that when we are happy and "flitting around," our mind is not on serious things at all! We easily forget the hardships of others, the sadness and grief of others. When we arrive in this place of blissful freedom, then we even forget our own past pains and hurts. We certainly will give no thought then of bitter times, of sad times, painful times, for we are caught up in the glory and excitement of our new found freedom.

When we start taking things for granted, loss is just ahead. It is the only way some will ever learn to appreciate their freedom. Freedom is to be a guarded and cherished thing. It does not happen at all times and to all peoples. Many do suffer and have suffered from the lack of freedom. When things come to us easily, they also leave easily.

Freedom is a lot like love. It brings great joy, great happiness and creative ability, a very quiet strength. Quiet strengths that never create strife and exude joy and happiness are the easiest to take advantage of and loose appreciation for. This is freedom.

There are many kinds of freedom in many areas. I like to think that American freedom granted by our constitution, and love granted to us by God are the two greatest freedom yielding forces in the world. Too often, many have had these and lost them. The thing to remember is this; no one who ever had either and lost them will ever forget that liberty and freedom they once had. Some can never have it again like it once was!!!

Appreciation for freedom, in whatever form it comes into our lives, is a fragile thing! Cherish it, fight for it, stand for it! Someone gave greatly and valiantly for us to experience the freedom we have in your country today. Many gave their lives for American freedom.

Christ gave his life for us to be able to experience real freedom, too. We can be free and experience emotional freedom also. There are many kinds of freedom to appreciate. Our Christian freedom is not the removal of moral restraints, but the freedom to serve one another! That was the first thing Constantine did. He removed the Christian's freedom to love one another by restricting their ability to serve their fellow man's needs.

Cherish your freedom wherever you find it for someone has paid a great price for you! *Now the Lord is the Spirit; and where the Spirit of the Lord is there is liberty!"*—2 Corinthians 3:17. This is most evident when our Lord is in our government, too!

Enjoy any freedom you have today, for freedom is born from love!!! Our soldiers fought and many died for it because they loved it and their families!

That is the cost and the value of freedom.
Let's keep it!!!

ETIQUETTE

"Isn't etiquette just to be considered in formal situations?"
you may ask.
No.

Proper etiquette seems to make some people very anxious when they are not sure if they are educated enough for the scene or the place. This is especially true if it is a place that is regarded as requiring impeccable behavior.

The heart and foundation of etiquette is not something that can be taught. It is actually as simple as thoughtfulness and consideration of others. Respect for others, their feelings and for their things would be another way our display of learned etiquette can be observed. A person who is well-mannered and behaving properly is a person who is kind and thoughtful of others feelings.

The very thoughtful are always well-mannered. Putting others' feelings above our own is sometimes all it takes to display good manners. A person who knows how to behave and is confident in it is known as a person who is polished and well bred.

What is considered good manners in one place may not be so in another place. Indeed it might be the opposite! Everyone should desire excellence in this area. Social etiquette differs from professional etiquette. Cultural etiquette is quite varied and possibly the easiest and most frequently misunderstood.

If you are unsure what the proper manner is for what you are going to be doing or where you want to go, I suggest you get a good book especially written for the situation. Protocol is also the proper conduct fitting into the right place and time.

Find someone who can teach you and ask them to help you learn the very basics of consideration and thoughtfulness of others. That is really what it is all about. If you are someone who respects others and their things, you are probably already a well-mannered person or child. However, if you do not feel confident of your knowledge, then you need to learn some good manners, good behavior, and this will make you confident! It is the thing that will cause the welcome mat to be offered to you in a person's life and in their home over and over again.

Again, if we observe the teachings of God in His word we will be successful in all we undertake to do:

Let nothing be done through selfish ambition or conceit, but in lowliness of mind let each esteem others better than himself. Let each of you look out not only for his own interests, but also for the interests of others—Philippians 2:3-4.

From manners to salvation, God covers it all with his knowledge. Find it, apply it, and be confident today!!!

I can hear it now, "They are so well-mannered!"
Another attribute of Holy Spirit!!! Amen?

THE KINGDOM LIFE

Is it really possible to live in God's Kingdom
while we're still on earth?

Where earthly kings and queens reign a kingdom is easily understood! Many like to believe they are in the kingdom as Nicodemus felt like he desired to be. We must have the kingdom of God in us before we can live each day in His kingdom.

When we get saved we get Jesus! We enter His kingdom life with death to self, as Jesus explained to Nicodemus. When we enter His kingdom, we do not just have Jesus, but now Jesus has "got us!!!"

To enter this kingdom living requires death to everything outside His kingdom. Nicodemus came by night (his darkness), into the light (the presence of Jesus) to receive truth. Many have done this and refused to pay the price of complete obedience to God.

Though Nicodemus did become an ardent disciple of Jesus, another rich, young ruler evidently did not. When Jesus told him what he must do to gain eternal life, he decided the price was too great and he walked away sorrowful. God never intended him give all he had away. He said he should sell his material goods and give to the poor. He, being a rich ruler, had means of income and had he complied he would have discovered everything given in obedience is returned, thirty, sixty, or a hundred fold.

Many today go away sorrowful, never entering into the blessed Kingdom Of God life. The rich, young ruler could not think into the spiritual realm, for he existed only with "good works," in the flesh, Luke 18:18-27. He had kept all the laws—all of the dos and don'ts, but without relationship. His only experience was the natural life, none of the spiritual life.

Every fleshly action of man results in a downward move and direction. Every action and move with God results in an upward movement. When Jesus used the wind as an example while talking to Nicodemus He lifted this Kingdom teaching from the natural to the spiritual realm (John 3:7-8). The blood forgives our sin, the water (The Word) **cleanses** us, and the Holy Spirit enables us to live above sin.

Sometimes we may fail as we learn to ascend higher and function in the realm of the spirit! The rich, young ruler knew about blood sacrifices, but being in the flesh did not understand the Word and the Holy Spirit. God wants to lift us higher, always He is calling us higher…come up higher…and live the Kingdom life! We see this in Revelation 4:1:

> *After these things I looked, and behold a door standing open in heaven. And the first voice which I heard was like a trumpet, (revelation), speaking with me saying, Come up here, and I will show you things which must take place after this! Immediately I was in the Spirit and behold a throne set in heaven, and One sat on the throne!"*

Our King is calling us to come higher, come with Him to higher places in the Spirit!

Are you responding with great anticipation and obedience or are you walking away sorrowfully?
Come up higher!!!

INTIMACY WITH FATHER

What is it to really know the Father?

And this is eternal life, that they may know You, the only true God, and Jesus Christ whom you have sent.... That they may be one, as You, Father are in Me, and I in You; that they also may be one in Us, that the world may believe that You sent Me—John. 17:3, 21.

This is indeed the prayer that Jesus prayed for us! The key word here is KNOW! If I know you I have key and first hand information about you and who you really and truly are. It's in the Father's heart that we desire to be living with Him intimately. Jesus is the door to get to this intimate place.

We learn to get there by reading what He wrote and abiding in a secret place where we meet with Him regularly and often. The more we learn of Him, the more we know Him, and the more we know Him, the greater the interpersonal relationship we may have. Humans have a spiritual need to belong and to love which the intimate relationship with the Father satisfies.

We are much more than physical—we are spiritual beings who receive life into our spirit when we are born again. When we are born as a human being, someone supplies our needs, our clothes, our food etc. When we are born again in Christ Jesus we receive the supplies we need from the Holy Spirit and our Father. We are given those things as we grow in need of them. We do this in the secret place where we spend time with Him getting to know our Father.

The quality of our relationship with Him and how much of our Father we posses is entirely up to us. We can have as much of Him and His time as we desire, sometimes much unlike an earthly father! He will keep on giving and giving of Himself into our lives as long as we desire Him and receive what He has for us.

We go to our Father who repairs us by forgiving us, He restores us by giving back to us and refreshing us. We intimately share our fears, our pain, and He heals us. He talks with us. Intimacy with the Father causes us to know the wonderful heavenly Father He really is!

This is a very close and affective relationship. Here we dialogue with Father, totally transparent, very vulnerable, but trusting and with reciprocity a very rewarding and loving relationship is developed. It is here we open our heart and our hidden thoughts and feelings we can now discuss with Him. He will become so close to those who seek Him that on-going conversations and dialogue with Him are as comfortable and as usual as conversations with another person!

In order for this intimate relationship to develop, you must come first to Jesus; be born again, then obey Father, recognizing Him as King over His kingdom. Ask Him to talk to you, reveal who He is to you! Spend time with Him, watch, listen and soon you will be in a personal relationship with the Creator of the Universe…just you and Him!!! Wow! Think about that!!!

It's a very, very exciting relationship!!!

MOTIVATION

The reason for doing something or behaving in a particular way.

There are many aspects of motivation. Let's just think about the area of the motives of the heart. This is key to all we do. God talked about it and reminded us that He is only interested in that part of our actions. We are either prompted by holy motives or fleshly, evil motives. There is no "in between" motive. When we understand ourselves we will also began to see our motives for doing things. When we see the motive we will change if it is not prompted by His holiness.

Understanding a person's motives is actually a greater depth of understanding them. "Church goers" really need to check their motives because a servants heart can very easily become the ambitious heart. The reason you started may not be the reason you are continuing. Many do not realize it, but if your heart is not right in what you are doing then your destiny is in a trap. If your motive is not right then you are a hindrance to the work and plan of God. Many things Christians do are not from a pure heart. Many women in the church are not "chasing God", they are "chasing the man of God" and chasing after an elusive future.

Our words, attitude, and actions not only reveal our motive, but also many times will uncover many hidden personal problems. Fortunately or unfortunately those with understanding and discernment see many of these motives which are very clearly exposed to them by their gifts. Time and conditions will certainly expose hidden motives.

Some people's motives speak so loudly you do not even need understanding to grasp them easily. Pride, arrogance, and self-centered people much of the time have motives they try to hide. A person who is entertaining an impure motive is definitely not submitted to the authority of God and His word. This is hidden rebellion in a heart with wrong motives.

What you look like, the clothes you wear, are not what God has been looking at or is interested in for, with your permission, He can change all of that. He is the Holy Spirit, a spirit is not interested in what you are wearing, a spirit by passes what you look like and the way you dress although the evil human spirit is most always fascinated by these two things.

God knows exactly what you are trying to do, what you are trying to say and the motive you are using to do it. No one has ever hidden their heart from God! It is an impossibility! Many of your motives you think are hidden are on open display most of the time.

Is the last thing you did what you were choosing to do because that is what YOU wanted to do?

Was the reason you did it or are doing it because IT IS what the Holy Spirit instructed you to do?

Why are you saying those things?

Why are you doing those things?

God knows and He either ordered it and appreciates it or you are on your on stalling your REAL destiny. You and God know "the why!"

The Lord said to Samuel, do not look at his appearance or at his physical stature because I have refused him. For the Lord does not see as man sees, for man looks at the outward appearance, but the Lord looks at the heart—1 Samuel 16:7.

What is it your eyes are looking at?

Where did your motive come from?

When your heart is right your destiny in God cannot be denied!

FRIEND?

Have you ever had a "best friend in all the world?"

A friend is that person who knows you and still likes you. A friend believes in you and what you want to achieve and will encourage you in every single good work you undertake to accomplish. A friend knows that it is not always words that need to be said but their presence to be felt and seen. A friend wants the very best for you and when it happens they are the first to become excited about your achievements.

There are two sides of timing to every friendship. There are the times you give and then there is the time you receive of that friend. It is important to know when it is a time as a friend to do either of these...give to that friendship or receive from it. Friends share the same enemies. A friend will defend you in your absence and will not tolerate the presence of someone in their life that is against you.

True friendship is a very rare blessing and escapes us when we do not appreciate it or cherish it. Friendship is like marriage, it is never a one way street. It requires the giving and taking, also. A friend is forever favoring you. Others around you will easily be able to see who your best friend is. A friend is a supporter, a comrade, a very special chum! Friends have been referred to as cronies, companions, side-kicks, and many other "pet names." What is important to you will also be very important to your friend!

I don't know about you, but I cannot "pretend" you are my friend. I will not ever do that. If I think of you, love you as a friend, and you break my trust in you, then I will forgive you. It may take me a few hours or a day or two, but I will forgive you. I then want no reminders of you and the pain you created in my life so I will be removing your pictures and all reminders of you from my life. I will not mistreat you nor will I gossip about you. I will not ever seek revenge for any hurt, neither in word or deed.

A friend is someone who loves with their whole heart and proves that love over and over as the years pass. If you are ever a true, true, friend you are a forever kind of friend. There are very, very few of these people in the world. In my opinion, I do not really believe you can be a great friend without being a Christian and obeying the Holy Spirit who resides in you. His principles in a friend who honors Him is the safety in the friendship.

Are you a true friend to anyone? Is there anyone who is really and truly a friend to you, tested and true? A true friend loves at all times!!! Be thankful to God for a true friend for they are one of the greatest blessings in your lifetime!

God can call you friend if you know the real meaning of that word!

A friend loveth at all times,
and a brother is born for adversity—Proverbs 17:17.

COVENANT

...a solemn agreement to engage in or to refrain from a specified action
...like our choice to enter into covenant with Christ Jesus.

This is the most important covenant we will ever receive and come into agreement with. I believe the second most important one is the Godmate that we enter into covenant agreement with. When we enter into the new covenant with Christ Jesus then that can make all our other covenants successful!

There are all kinds of covenants with all kinds of names. There is the Abrahamic covenant, Davidic covenant, covenantal theology, (Roman Catholic). There is also the Mosaic covenant. This is the eternal covenant between God and Israel. (In this, the Shabbat, or Sabbath, is declared to be the sign forever.)

Then of course the most important one where Jesus Christ is the mediator and the old Mosaic covenant is replaced by His new covenant sealed with His death and resurrection. This is our covenant as Christians with an almighty God whose blood in His death for the entire human race has NEVER lost its power to save and redeem!

All covenants are very significant and should not be entered into without much prayer and serious thought! God is very serious about covenants, our words of promise, our pledges, our debts—all are covenants which we have entered into. Anytime we enter into agreement with another, written or spoken, it is a covenant. It is serious. It is our word which ultimately becomes part of our integrity and even our character!

The most important thing to remember about a covenant is this: Our Father God takes each one very seriously and we should do the very same thing! God said, *Whatever we bind on earth is bound in heaven!*" That is serious!!! He told us, *I have made a covenant with My chosen, I have sworn unto David My servant. My covenant will I not break, nor alter the thing that is gone out of My lips*—Psalm 13:12.

Father God takes our covenant so seriously He even warned us: *Take heed unto yourselves, lest ye forget the covenant of the Lord your God, which He made with you, and make you a graven image, or the likeness of thee."* (Likeness of thee....that is self!) *"For the Lord thy God is a consuming fire, even a jealous God*—Deuteronomy 4:23-24!

If we do not have a healthy fear of God we will not be able to keep our covenant with our Almighty God. If we do fear God and walk in His ways we will grow in favor with God and man...

Increasing and increasing and increasing!!!

OCCUPATION

What is your "occupation?"

Some may call it work, career or calling. I call it occupation for that is exactly what it is. Jesus said, "*Occupy until I come.*" That means continue to work the work you should be doing.

I have often heard that the word work to some is a dirty word. This is simply because they are lazy and without any dreams for themselves or those around them! Work to them then, is a drudgery because it interferes with their love of only enjoying the fruit of everyone else's labor around them.

Look seriously at your work today. Is it just a place you occupy and a place where you are just spending your time; your entire life? Is it a career? Is it what God designed you to do? Sometimes the answers to these questions cannot be had real easily.

Maybe you did not even choose your occupation. Maybe your parents chose it for you, maybe you feel like it is the only thing that you are educated to do. Maybe your motive for doing what you are doing is what is driving you.

Is that motive God, or for God?

We all know whether we invent or build something new or manage something that already exists, that we are going to need certain things and certain people to do specified things. God knew this when He created the universe and our Earth on which we live. He looked ahead in time and saw what the need was; the problems that would exist, so He created what would be needed to solve those problems.

It is up to us to discover these things. We do that in the secret place, alone with the Holy Spirit, godly counsel, and obeying Him in each thing we do. One of those things created is a person—you! Just like He knew we would need coal, oil, etc. for energy and warmth, you were created for a purpose. Have you found it or are you just working because you need to?

There is a place where you fit in, and a place that will explode with success with you there. You, yourself, will be happy there and WANT to get to that place each day and hate to leave it! Dr. Mike Murdock says that if there were no problems then you would not be necessary! You are the answer to a problem somewhere and you are the perfect answer for that problem! God is so perfectly intelligent that He will take all the places that you have worked that He did not call you to and weave them right into that place, for He knew one day you would want to do what He created you to do!

When the Creator and the created are in agreement, there is perfect peace. God's divine plan and the plan for your life are divinely fitted together! You can find that place. It is the place God designed you to be successful in occupying! The Holy Spirit will lead you there if you are submitted to Him. There is money and provision waiting for you there. There is also peace to go with the prosperity. "The problems you solve determine the reward you receive," Dr. Mike Murdock.

The Word tells us:

And I will multiply upon you man and beast; and they shall increase and bring fruit: and I will settle you after your old estates, and will do better unto you than at your beginnings; and ye shall know that I am the Lord, **Ezekiel 36:11.**

Know where you belong today for the plan is eternal! You can!!!

SACRIFICES

Much, much, could be said about sacrifices and sacrificing.

Behind every successful accomplishment, every powerful anointing, you will find sacrifice, pain, and suffering. (It is my opinion since God loves His children so much that after He has watched us sacrifice and be faithful He will not permit anyone to come against us and our anointing.) If those painful sacrifices had not taken place in the lives of the Sons of God, then we would not be able to receive all that God has for us!

Sacrifice is not what some may think. I will not attempt to write here all that the word sacrifice includes and covers in our lives. A Christian mother's love will cause her to sacrifice her life for her children. However, unfortunately, we now see mothers sacrificing their children's very lives for what they desire. Are we losing sight of what a real sacrifice is? Of sacrificial love for God?

A sacrifice is not what you simply gave up, not what you lost in a divorce, death, fires, or maybe a bankruptcy because of asinine judgment or poor choices. A sacrifice cannot be a sacrifice that is significant to God unless it is with true devotion. Many people sacrifice things every day just because they want to do something that they are desiring to do. If it is not sacrificed for the right purpose, it is not a godly sacrifice! It is wasted on things that will perish rather than on building eternal things, establishing the Kingdom of God. Isaiah told us this in chapter one, Empty-hearted sacrifice and soulless worship is not true devotion.

True sacrifice is the ordained way to approach God. Some of these appointed ways are in prayer, corporate worship, and also, forgiveness. The greatest sacrifice of all time, past—present—and future, was the sacrifice of the life of Jesus, the sacrificial Lamb, once and for all, that removes sin of the world, John 1:29 and Hebrews 10:10!

The rich young ruler was not willing to sacrifice and because of that he knew he could not have what he so desired. He walked away already sorrowful for the loss he now felt. When God calls, it will always be a sacrifice to leave this world and all that is involved therein behind.

Sometimes the sacrifice that is required is not something that was bad for us. Sometimes it is the very thing that brought us great joy and happiness. Even though it is not bad for us, there is not room for it or that person, where God is taking us. However, we cannot out give God. He said He will give us back in this lifetime and in the life to come much, much more than we ever sacrificed for Him. It is truly a test to give all to the Lord—then trust—wait to see how He will multiply it and give it back to us!

A sacrifice is a willing offering to our God. It is an attitude of the heart. Anything less perverts the real purpose of the sacrificial system and is unacceptable to God.

What are you sacrificing and is it an ordained sacrifice or one you are making simply for something you want to do or accomplish?

The sacrifices of God are a broken spirit, a broken and a contrite heart, these O God You will not despise!

Psalm 51:17.

King David's words say it all.

INSPIRATION

Inspiration…even the sound of the word is beautiful.

I believe that it is no accident because, everything associated with the word 'inspiration', and/or 'inspirational' denotes happiness and beauty.

God wanted us to know that He inspired His Word so that it became something that comes alive in us. Sharper than a sword to cut at flesh. What divine inspiration!

Inspiration, it seems to me, is divine guidance from the immediate influence of God, Himself. I have always said that inspiration is the mind of God touching the heart of a man. The heart is the real man, it is what makes him who he is. When inspiration touches his heart, it touches his mind and then it will begin to be seen in the physical.

The sight of some particular individual can inspire us, as can words, an act, or even something we have seen. The Spirit and the God-life in someone can inspire us to more godly things. When we see a picture created by a word, an act, a thought, a sight—that mental picture immediately affects us. If we control that which affects us then we can control our inspiration.

There are individuals who themselves are an inspiration for they seem to just radiate inspiration as they carry the Glory of God. We should know those who stir our spirits, stir us to greater than what we thought we could be. I like the song, "You Raise Me Up To More Than I can Be!" In other words, you are my inspiration for greater achievement in my life.

People who carry this God touch...the breathing in of God into our lives... are just really awesome to be around, and their value is far beyond words. They can be the reason you get to your next goal or that long lost dream. The inspiration they create just causes it to happen! I like to imagine breathing in the breath of God and aspiring to the greatest of heights! As I literally breathe God in, a smile erupts from my face! I cannot hide what God thoughts do for me...for they are great inspirations for me each day—often many times a day!!!

Inspiration is of God! We can be quietly drifting along and all of a sudden our spirit, mind, and then our body becomes lifted to a much higher place by an immediate influence of the God touch! The scripture could not be what it has been, remaining even to this day, without the inspiration of God upon the mind and heart of the writers. God does not override our intellect and sensitivity, but He touches it with His influence of inspiration and then we are suddenly off and running!!!

God knows how to "regulate" and "maintain" what he created! Everything good in our lives came from a godly influence, recognized or not! Read 1 Corinthians 2:6-12 right now and be inspired!!!

> *Now we have received, not the spirit of the world, but the Spirit who is from God, that we might know the things that have been freely given to us by God*!!!

I get so excited just thinking about the greatness, the

sweetness, the power, the inspiration of our Mighty God! We are serving a God Who knows no limits in anything of greatness!!!

Am I excited?

You know I am!!!

Real excited!!!

I hope you are too!!!

PEACE PART 2

> "Peace like a river is gently flowing"…..
> (the words to an old song!)

Peace moves in and around our lives like a powerful and smooth running river! Great is its depths and strength. When the outside world sees peace in the life of a person where there seems to be no explanation for it, the peace becomes a witness.

Peace does not come or stay because of outside circumstances or influences. Many times we allow those things to steal our peace! We do not have to do that! Jesus is our peace—always—and He never leaves the inside of us for He has come to take up permanent residence there if we will allow Him to. The world can only give you "surface "peace", temporary peace. It does not last.

There is actually no way to explain the peace of God to anyone for God told us in His word that His peace will pass all understanding! It does! Peace reigns in the pure heart, the heart that is walking in favor, both with God and man. Peace rests in the pure heart, in the trusting heart, in the security of knowledge and belief in who one's God is.

Disturbance and strife are not known in the heart that

is at peace. When we find who we are in Christ a great depth of peace begins to reign in our heart. When we walk in the spirit, (and if we are walking in the spirit we are indeed walking in love), then the peace of God flows to us and through us!

Many people who walk in this abundance of peace carry this great spiritual blessing right into the atmosphere and environment around them! It can immediately be felt! When we are in a harmonious and godly relationship, there we will find the evidence of serenity and tranquility.

God spoke much about peace. We must be careful how we approach a person who dwells in peace when offering them new information, sad information, or bad news. The reason for this is simple...you are entering a peaceful world of thought in them that may shatter their world temporally. Approach a peaceful person with news in a peaceful manner. A quiet peaceful mind should be recognized and honored in this way!

When we begin to lose our peace—we have lost our way in a given situation. We may feel the loss of peace in something that has yet to be revealed to us—something our spirit has recognized, yet our minds have not received. Loss of peace should always be noted. God said follow the path of peace. It simply means that we are walking without strife in the way our Father has led us or instructed us!

Peace is a great benefit of our salvation! We need not be concerned about tomorrow! "Peace is not the absence of conflict, it is the absence of inner conflict."—one of Dr. Mike Murdock's Wisdom Keys for peace.

Thou wilt keep him in perfect peace, whose mind is stayed on Thee: because he trusteth in Thee.... Lord, thou wilt ordain peace for us: for Thou also has wrought all our works in us—Isaiah 26:3, 12.

Singing—I go along life's road, praising my Lord and walking in peace!

Feel this great peace today...
this is an impartation of peace for you!!!
Receive it!!!

UNDERESTANDING

Do you understand "understanding?"

Any kind of a relationship we have will require this word many times. We need to seek understanding of the words of God, of others, and of circumstances. God said, With all our getting, to get understanding!

Many people who do not spend much time thinking are also the same ones who are void of understanding many times. Understanding requires meditation and thinking on a given subject in order for real understanding to come. How shall we truly comprehend the meaning of God's words or those of others, if we do not understand the words, the people, the circumstances? Without proper understanding of things and people we cannot possibly come to intelligent decisions or conclusions.

Understanding is a blessing that must be pursued in order to really know the meaning and wishes of others. Pride sometimes keeps us from learning something that we really may need to know because we will not say the statement, "I do not understand."

Sometimes understanding requires more information than we already have. We must seek that information in some way in order to arrive at what understanding of something really is. There is no way that you will arrive at the proper understanding of a thing without questions. Questions help us to understand. Of course we must know that questions to understand are not the same questions that are asked just to know another's business. Those are just "nosy questions."

The motive for asking questions should be to find enough information so that understanding can be birthed. Conversation is necessary to arrive at right understanding. People who are afraid to ask the right questions will not be the person who readily understands. Without proper information it cannot happen.

Discernment helps us to understand, but discernment and understanding do not have the same meanings. When we are blessed with a mate or a friend who understands us it becomes a double blessing for both. Understanding births peace and security in relationships. If I know why you do things or the reasoning behind why you do things, then I will have no need of so much patience. I simply understand.

Understanding why a person does something does not mean that we approve of what they do, either. When we know we have the understanding of another we feel a safety. Experience has taught us that "the time" that will make us feel the craziest and very much alone is when we think no one understands us. Some people are just not easy to understand, so few will take the time to understand.

We could know God better if we would study His ways more and come to a greater understanding of how He really does work in our lives. We need understanding and we need it every single day in order to live more peacefully! The more we understand each other the more depths our relationship can have!

God said that, "the entrance of His words was a light, giving understanding to the simple." Understanding births much freedom in many areas. I love "understanding and wisdom" and what God says about it!

In the lips of him that hath understanding wisdom is found; but a rod is for the back of him that is void of understanding—Proverbs 10:13.

Always find wisdom where you have found understanding! If it required understanding for God to build the heavens, surely it is required for us to build anything!

Wisdom is the principle thing;
therefore get Wisdom;
and with all they getting get understanding.
Proverbs 4:7

Understanding will birth patience!

CHANGE

Many people say they do not like change—Do you?

"Change Is Always Proportionate to your knowledge," a Wisdom Key of my mentor, Dr. Mike Murdock. Such a true statement of change. Think about that...it is profound!!

Knowledge can be profound and with that can come profound change. Everyone is going through change. Everyone has gone through change—many times in life. People change around us. Things change around us. Seasons change and we must decide what changes we need to make to adapt to the new season.

Change always brings "the new"—something we have not ever experienced! If we are changing we are growing. If we are learning we are growing. When we stop changing we began to die. We must always aspire to greater heights in all things. The more knowledge that comes into our lives the greater the changes that will take place.

We say that older people are "too set in their ways to change." We know why that is...they have lost the desire for learning "the new," so nothing new is happening in their lives. They have begun to lose life rather than preserving what they have and gaining new "leases on life" by changes.

There are mentors and teachers who can bring great change—great growth into our lives by their words and by their knowledge imparted to us. Listening is the seed for learning and learning is the seed for change.

When we give our lives to Christ we are changed from the old into the new man. Christ alone is the one who brings a man into change as He moves him in his knowledge. Knowledge of Christ changes men. This is the purpose of teaching—change! Change can come suddenly, it can come quickly, slowly—even without a notice.

Questions are the seed for knowledge and knowledge will change us. It is safe to say that if our knowledge is growing we are most definitely changing. If we desire to change in any area, all we have to do is seek the knowledge of that area or subject—apply it—and we will begin changing. Knowledge—for sure—changes us!

Take serious and earnest thought about any time or effort you are spending obtaining worthless knowledge in readings and conversations. If it is not something that will improve and increase your knowledge for good then it will not bring good changes. The more knowledge you obtain the more change—of course—you will experience. This is why parents seek to shield their children from certain knowledge, for it will cause negative growth in areas of their mind—then their lives!

And have put on the new man, which is renewed in knowledge after the image of Him that created him—Colossians 3:10.

Always remember that change will require adaptation which may put a demand on your knowledge!

Change creates many different things!!!

PRAYER

Prayer...one of my favorite places to be.

It is here that I can remain in the presence of my Father. I never want to leave His presence. If I could stay there forever I would! Prayer is a very intimate time for me with my Father. It is no different than my most intimate relationship here on earth except it is full scope in intimacy and trustworthiness in a so much higher level! It is here I tell my Father all my feelings about everything. He knows me well.

I have need to hide nothing from Him. Not even those imperfections and weaknesses, for He knows them all and loves me anyway. He never scolds me or turns His back on me. He is always waiting for me to come to Him and I love the way He accepts me, just exactly the way I am!

I sing to Him and He sings with me and then it becomes a beautiful concerto! I praise Him for His goodness to me, His holiness...so beautiful, and His faithfulness that never fails. As I praise Him, He becomes excited in His heart for me and I feel Him lifting me up from where I was when I met Him this day. He lifts all things too heavy for me to carry and takes them Himself so I am no longer burdened and feeling cast down.

He smiles at me and tells me how much He loves me. My trust in Him and His sweet love for me makes me know I can wait in safety for Him to do things with me and for me. I have no desire to do it my way...I just want to do it His way and make Him happy! I am sad when I know I have tried to do it my way, and in not seeking His counsel I broke His heart for He had something better for me than what I achieved myself. I learned to wait for Him.

In my thinking and decisions there before Him, all becomes clear and I see my direction. I then remember that He is helping me stay on the right path! I know if I will acknowledge Him, He will direct my path. He sees that I come with gratitude and thanksgiving in my heart and in my life for He has been good to me all the days of my life! He is a good Father!

I always come before my Father with thanksgiving, praise and my songs to Him. He always is there waiting to get closer to me. He wants to be close to me and I have such desire for Him! He knows it and He so desires what I give Him in my adoration of Him. It is not a time where I am asking for things of Him, except for those three things, it is just enjoyment of Him and His presence!

Anyone can have an intimate relationship with our Father—It is simply called praying. It is called spending time alone with Him so our relationship can grow deeper! I love Him so!

He truly is my shepherd! I do not want! He restores me! He comforts me! I have no need of fear! He anoints me and my cup of joy runs over! He blesses me in the presence of my enemies and causes them to see I am favored by my Heavenly Father! *...He leads me in the paths of righteousness for His name's sake*—Psalm 23:3.

I cannot explain my relationship with my Father except to say it is intimate, so loving and so satisfying! My words fail when it comes to describing and being in the presence of love! He is like liquid love poured out over me and in my life!!!

There is not enough time or space to describe my Beloved!

He is my favorite person to write about!

SIMPLICITY

Have you ever considered the beauty of simplicity?

Not much thought is given to simplicity. Life and all things in it have become complex and without simplicity so much appreciation of it has been lost and some recognition also! I pray that is not true of you. I hope you have just kept it simple, for if you have you will also find simplicity is "akin" to real. Very much so!

Simplicity of person is an absence of show or pretense. It is raw sincerity. There is no slither in simplicity. As someone has said, "What you see is what you get." Jesus made no pretenses about anything. He didn't even make the choice to follow Him complex. He was bold and straight forward about the cost. His words were simple, yet profound.

Most things that are profound are made so with simplicity. Simplicity is our God undiscovered. God is very complex and oh what complex wisdom, what a complex mind! Yet He speaks and acts in such profound simplicity that we miss Him many, many times. I am not talking about a person here who is a simple minded person. I am talking about the essence of the person, the simplicity of His nature.

One of the reasons the Holy Spirit is so capable of quickly humbling us is with His clear and concise words of simplicity with accuracy. Simplicity could hide on a stage in Madison Square Garden! I have had the honor of witnessing several lives of simplicity two of which you may also have known or do know today. One is Billy Graham and the other is my Pastor, Dr. Mike Murdock.

Those who live in simplicity—yet greatness—will quickly recognize it in other people. A person of simplicity is the one who understands his purpose in this world is to help people by serving our God in obedience to His word and laws. A simple hearted person is one where we see an unaffected nature and exuding no guile but always living and breathing sincerity.

Simplicity in the unaffectatious person is most always likeable but without the other person really understanding why. This person is a gatherer because of this! Just like Jesus was always a gatherer. The best thought of a heart of simplicity is in this scripture: *Let nothing be done through selfish ambition or conceit, but in lowliness of mind let each esteem others better than himself*—Philippians 2:3.

No matter how you describe it whether it be "down to earth" or sincere, the fact remains simple…so many times…
  …Simplicity is our God…
  unrecognized!!!

RECEIVING

Much, much time I have spent in thinking and studying on this word.
There are all kinds of receiving, from a personal gift to the business of receiving.

There are receivers who are appointed by courts of law for different reasons. Some are for things that are in dispute. Then there are court appointed receivers for things that are in transit through the court system. These receivers are charged with managing and preserving what they are charged with receiving. Receivers are most always granted wide powers. NO ONE is appointed to be a receiver who is not qualified to take charge of what becomes known as receivership of cases or items they receive whatever it may be. These receivers need to be in the position to welcome these wide powers so granted to them. This is a good description of true receiving.

Our God is also one who appoints us to receive. I have come to a conclusion that in order to receive what God has for us there is a seed that must be sown. It is the seed of trust. I believe that trust is indeed the seed for a harvest of receiving. I believe this is why many do not receive their harvest or their answers to prayer.

Once we fully understand the word "receive," then we see that how we receive often does not indicate a great receiver. Self-centered people, selfish and greedy people will receive with excitement and enthusiasm. There is a lot of difference between getting something and receiving something. Most always, receiving from man does not require trust. This kind of receiving only requires a desire to have.

With God it is a different story altogether. I have been in great spiritual services of wonderful impartation and saw that only a very few actually received what was offered or imparted. Receiving from God requires trust on our part and I believe God looks for it each time He wants to impart something to us. He does not give His power gifts to all people! It requires trust. Trust that He knows we will not abuse. He must know He can trust our tongue and our conduct with His power.

God trusted His Son, Jesus, as we see in Matthew 3:17, Luke 9:35 and 2 Peter 1:17. We cannot receive salvation until we trust in the cross and death of Jesus to save us. We see in Psalm 24 that in order to receive the honor of standing in the Holy Place, requires holiness that God can trust in to place us there.

Unbelief will not respond to truth, therefore there is no seed of trust for receiving from our God.

The reason many never receive and change after hearing the teaching is because they are doubting that God sent teacher. Paul gave instructions to the Philippians about Epaphroditus so they could trust in him, therefore they could receive him and his gifts. See Philippians 2:25-30.

This article could become longer than we have time to read! The word of God is full of the fact that in order to receive we must be qualified with trust in our authority and toward our God. We cannot become a true son of God if we have not sown the life that God can trust in.

Receiving is a two way street! God trusts me with receiving it and I am trusting God that I am going to get it from Him.

But as many as received Him to them He gave the power, (right). to become the sons of God; to those who believe in his name—John 1:12.

In James He says to us…if you doubt me, (have not sown the seed of trust), then expect to receive nothing!!!

Trust is the seed for the harvest of receiving!!!

DECEPTION PART 2

And Jesus answered and said unto them, "Take heed that no man deceive you."

As we read this we know right away that we have been warned. Deception brings with it great disappointment once truth has been revealed. Eve was the first to be deceived by giving time to satan in a conversation. The purpose of his conversation was to create enough doubt in her that she actually became an unbeliever right there in the garden.

Many people listen to the wrong people and become deceived. Some are deceived because they have begun to believe their own desires are those of Christ Jesus for them. What we want is in the flesh, what God wants for us is in His spirit. Our flesh will rarely agree with the Holy Spirit. We will deny and argue and try to find peace in that by which we are deceived, but peace never comes concerning it.

We will try to groom ourselves and change ourselves for that position for which we are deceived into believing is what God wants. Many have wasted entire lives chasing that which God has not given them. They have no life except the pursuit of that which is only a figment of their imagination in their spirit of deception. Many times revelation of truth will not be accepted and now it is too late for that which they could have done.

Some do not want to hear the truth and will never ask the Holy Spirit this question, "What is the purpose of this position, friendship, or this person in my life?" Therefore rather than hear the truth from God and accept it, they blindly go walking on in deception thinking all is well.

You can be deceived if you do not know your own self. You will be deceived if you do not know the scriptures. You will be deceived if you do not seek the truth about these things instead of trying to find someone who agrees with you in your deception. Deception always looks for someone to agree with it hoping it will bring peace, but peace does not come. (Moses sister sought someone to agree with her.)

Sometimes all it takes is a question, but few want to ask that question because they want to continue believing what they want is what is going to occur. You can know today and doubt no more. Ask for truth. Ask it of the individual. Ask it of God. Ask it of the word of God. If all of these do not line up then we know we are deceived.

Deception is great illusion and never real, fact, or truth. Women deceive themselves about men. They keep hoping things will change. They keep hoping "God" will turn things around for them when God is not even in it. They even pray for this and God is not in it at all. Men are deceived about women many times because they are trusting themselves and think they can change this person. They can change no one and neither can we.

Christians sit and listen to wrong teachings and not knowing the word of God—they become deceived. Children learn to believe lies and they become lost from truth by the spirit of deception.

People are deceived by politicians. If we sought the truth in who of these running for office paid their tithes—just even last year—much, much, would be exposed in those who run for office and call themselves Christians.

Deception is everywhere! *There is nothing covered, that shall not be revealed; neither hid, that shall not be known*—Luke 12:2.

No one has to be deceived!

IMAGINATION

I just love that word!

It is the golden key out of any place, any situation, at any time! Imagination is the seed that is so pregnant with dreams and life! Imagination can take you to worlds yet unknown, but oh, it can be so full of reality!

Imagination allows you to pre-play an event, then replay it again and again, then, if it happens, replay it some more!!! Increase the add-ons and let your imagination soar!

Not everything imagined can happen—not everything that is imagined will happen. Dreamers on the other hand many, many times make those imaginations come to reality in their lives!

We can have divine imagination or we can have evil imagination. If our imagination lines up with God's desires for us and our lives and His plans—then it is divine!!! It is a beautiful thing…the divine imagination! Imagination allows us to live an event many times! I believe that God was trying to get Abraham to imagine, even all down through the years even into his future of what would become of his seed.

God paints pictures for us. He shows us a vision of ourselves, closes that curtain then says, "Let's get busy where you are." Then you will forever be imagining that; like Abraham! God wanted Abraham to get his divine imagination working so he would be inspired to move on in the today!!! He did this when he was in a place that only his imagination could enable him to escape from; it was divine imagination!

Dreams come from the heart of God and God inspires man's mind to imagine around those dreams! I am a dreamer, and great is the imaginations of the dreamer! Imagination is the greatest key of escape ever! Imagination is what we are capable of believing! A person who is imagining is the person who is painting for himself, and perhaps for his future, the mental picture of what can be or what he knows he will make it to become.

Imagination is the key that unlocks the door of the prison. Imagination can help you to start seeing the size of our God.

Evil thoughts can be planted in our minds to birth evil imaginations which are designed to defeat us in mind battles. Never host evil imaginations! If not of God they are very destructive in all aspects. Words from poets, writers— pictures from artists can captivate our imagination until it soars into inspiration! Imagine that dream coming true, imagine the days, the nights and the new thing God is doing in our life, in our environment, in our country and in the world!

> "*No longer shall your name be called Abram, but your name shall be Abraham; for I have made you a father of many nations*!—Genesis 17:5.

Imagine that! Imagine..."*I will never leave you or forsake you!*" God's words to Joshua! Imagine...He told Jacob..."*your descendents cannot be numbered for multitude."* Imagine that!!! To Mary, *"behold you will conceive in your womb and bring forth a Son, and shall call his name Jesus!"* Imagine that! Luke 1:31.

Their imaginations must have soared beyond comprehension! We are living out the imaginations of these great ones, our own, and the Word of our God to them!!! Are you doing a great job today as their descendent...are you being faithful to our Divine forefathers imaginations and promises of our God to them and to us? Imagine that!!!

What are you capable of believing...
that is your imagination!
Be real sure its divine!!!

FAITHFULNESS

One who is faithful is the one who is worthy of trust!

Consistency is the hint that faithfulness may be found in us. The faithful never forsakes his duty in living and doing what is right. The faithful are full of faith and it is recognized in their accuracy in words and ways. The faithful one is one that brings joy and peace for they will be the cause of good things. Faithfulness eliminates doubt.

Sometimes it seems easier to describe what an unfaithful person says and does than to try to explain the faithful one.

Faithfulness is actually, in my opinion, proven goodness. Faithfulness is also a seed for hope. If you are faithful, I can safely put my hopes in you and know beyond a doubt you will be there for me. Coming to the conclusion that a person is faithful is truly a "time" process. It takes time for a person to prove themselves with faithfulness and to be found trustworthy!

The person who is not faithful will fail in their duty, break promises. You will soon learn they are fickle, doubting, skeptical, inconsistent and unreliable. Nobody wants to be any of these things, yet we do it every day in simply not keeping a promise. If we said it, then it should be known that it is as good as already done in the ear of our listener. We can depend on the faithful for they will be constant with truth.

God loves the faithful, for He tells us He preserves the faithful. His eye is on them and they will dwell with Him. God says man will proclaim his own goodness, so He asks us, who can find the faithful one? (Proverbs 20:6). God says blessed will be the faithful servant when He comes. I believe that means He acknowledges the faithful one in the here and now also!

God qualifies us for His true riches by our faithfulness with material things (Luke16:11). Lydia said in Acts that only those who deemed her faithful could come to her house.

Faithfulness is extremely important. Faithful people are hard to find and this is even true in our own homes and families. This is because people do not think that what we are doing now is what we shall account for in the great day of our God.

Paul made sure that the ones he sent to churches were known by him to be faithful. He said this of Timothy. Paul wrote the book of Colossians to the faithful. Read it as a faithful one and the words become rhema words to us!

The word says Moses was *"faithful in all his house."* That meant all of his life and that which surrounded him. He foreshadowed the One who was to come in his faithfulness.

It is so significant and important to God that we be faithful! He has explained to us that such a person receives the crown of life! It does not get any better than that. A faithful person exudes life in all its aspects while on this earth as well.

Without faithfulness in our Lord, how could we have hope? Are you faithful to God and man in ALL things?

His Lord said to him, well done, good and faithful servant; you have been faithful over a few things, I will make you ruler over many things. Enter into the joy of the Lord!—Matthew 25:23.

We are all servants,
but are we all the faithful servant who never even misses
the small things?
In the end that IS ALL that will matter!
Be blessed, faithful one!!!

THE CUP—THE PRAYER

Thank you, Jesus, for your blood.
Our life is in Your cup.
Your cup is our life.

This cup is royal and it flows through our veins as we become one royal family in You, with only one type of blood. The cup that tore the veil in two is the cup that gives us the right, now, to come into the Holy of Holies. We come now to give You gratitude for what You said to us, for what You did for us. You clearly told us, "*Life is in the blood.*"

Your blood has dispelled all darkness and made it possible for us to really see Your truth and what You have told us about this cup. You spoke to us in John 19:28 and You said, "*I thirst!*"

Jesus, we see why you are so thirsty. You could not drink of the cup that we drink of because no Nazarite was ever to taste of the fruit that came from the vine with its roots grown in the earth, the dust. We are Your new wine, the fruit, pressed into the vat to become one, Your bride, the wine that You will drink in that day of the marriage supper of the Lamb! Of this new wine You will drink.

Thank You, Father, that you are helping us to become this poured out wine, the wine You desire. You told us to "D*rink all of it!*" We must drink all of it so that we will not find ourselves sorrowing. Your true followers have always drunk deeply of Your cup, even as You drank all of Your cup. Even when You gave up Your will when You saw Your cup was not to pass, it was to drink, and You drank all. We drink all.

Help us Father as we seek You to be enabled to "drink all!" We know we are the new wine that in that day You will partake of, the new wine You will drink. We know that every single longing, every desire, the deeper things of You, the hunger, we will be filled to overflow in the day of that great celebration of the marriage supper of the Lamb.

You will drink of that new wine that we have become, and we will be eternally satisfied in our thirst for You and You for us. Communion—complete intimacy in that day!

Oh how we thank You and appreciate the understanding of Your words to us! We receive today Father, the greater knowledge of Your words, "I thirst."

And He took the cup, and gave thanks, and gave it to them, saying, Drink ye all of it; for this is My blood of the new testament, which is shed for many for the remission of sins. But I say unto you, I will not drink henceforth of this fruit of the vine, until that day when I drink it new with you in My Father's kingdom!—Matthew 26:27-29.

Father help us to see that You desire as much for us to be one with thee as we desire to be one with You. May we become the answer to Jesus' prayer:

"*Father make them one even as You and I are one.*"

In the sweet name, Christ Jesus, we pray.

OUR BREAD—THE BLESSING

"Take, eat. This is My body broken for you."

Father, we are so grateful today that as we feed on You, the Bread from Heaven, we become *partakers of Your divine nature* (2 Pet.1:4). As we receive You—our precious life-giving source—our souls are strengthened, healing comes to our lives, and this serves to testify of our faith in you.

Thank you that you came into this world as a symbol of bread lying in a manager, a place for eating, a lowly birth which tells of Your humility, yet with royal blood and with the richness of royalty and divinity. You, our precious bread, sustain us. Thank You, that anywhere in the world we can say bread and people know what we are saying. Bread, like music, or a smile is understood in all lands. We recognize that was Your divine plan from the beginning.

You were broken so we could be mended. Your body was broken as a symbol of broken bread that we can share You, our bread, with others. You allowed Your body to be captured so we could walk free of all bondages and captivity. Thank You, for the stripes which heal all our sicknesses and diseases. Because of that we can walk in heavenly health.

You endured the shame so we could believe in you and never be ashamed of Your gospel truths. You took our poverty—the curse, trading it for prosperity and divine riches with the crown of thorns on Your head. Thank You that as you willingly let your hands and feet be stilled with nails, You set our hands free to bless and our feet to walk in dominion over all earthy things.

We declare again today, You are The Lamb of God that washes us white as snow, without spot or wrinkle. Grant us unity, Father, that we all may become one kind of bread. The Bread of Life, sharing, multiplying Your life into the lives of others as we all become one with You.

In Christ Jesus' name we ask.
Amen.

Now Father, we cannot live by bread alone, and with that thought we remember...not bread alone but by every word from Your mouth... we say as others did in John 6:34-35:

Then said they unto Him, Lord, evermore give us this bread. And Jesus said unto them, I am the bread of life; he that cometh to Me shall never hunger; and he that believeth on Me shall never thirst."

We bless you, Jesus, our Bread today!!!

DUPLICITY

Duplicity... actually just a different name for a hypocrite!

The word does encompass more than just that of a hypocrite. There are people who are guilty of duplicity in business dealings as well. These, on purpose, saying and doing and signing things that are not honest, but are full of duplicity.

Seldom do we hear this word spoken of in the church but it would make a good topic for a Holiness preacher! Actually, the word of God tells us that beauty is deceitful. I think that could **apply** to many things including beautiful, flowering plants but whose blooms or leaves are poisonous. It could be applied to a "deal" that looks so good it is almost unbelievable. Maybe that is where the old saying came from, "It just sounds too good to be true!"

When God gives us something it is good and the joy that it brings to us sometimes makes us feel like it is unbelievable, but it is all true and from God!!! Anything that is not truth is a lie. Duplicity is when we try to make it a lie and truth too. This is what con-artist do many times to make themselves more believable. They use duplicity. Part of what they say is a truth, the other part is a lie. We hear that truth and many times, because we know it is a truth, somehow we become inclined to believe it all.

If you are pretending to entertain one set of intentions while acting under the influence of another then you are guilty of this sin of duplicity. If you are speaking or acting in two different ways concerning the same matter with intent to deceive you are guilty of this sin of duplicity. Those who are deceived will act in duplicity. It is simply a sustained form of deception which consist of entertaining or pretending to entertain one feeling and acting as if influenced by another bad faith.

Duplicity is a twofold state of evil and it surely is hypocritical. God requires honesty in the most inward parts, to others about others and in our heart about ourselves. If we are trying to live the Christian life, yet are dishonest in our heart about ourselves and our own heart then we are guilty of duplicity and are only deceiving ourselves with it. If we are Christians there should be nothing but straight truth in all we do and say!

Let love be without hypocrisy, abhor what is evil.
Cling to what is good!
Romans 12:9.

LAUGHTER

Refreshing as a trickling stream!

Ho, Ho, Ho....we even like the sound that is supposed to be the sound that Santa makes! Only the very sick and **depressed** cannot stand the sound of merriment. A merry heart is a heart that is full of smiles and laughter. I believe the joyful noise unto the Lord includes the sound of laughter.

I know God laughs for He has said funny things to me that caused me to laugh. Sometimes He is so simple in His speaking to us that it even makes us laugh. Sarah laughed and that is what her son's name came to mean!

Laughter is definitely the best medicine! That's because it is God's medicine—divine and supernatural medicine that even science has tried to explain. Laughter stimulates our respiratory system, our blood receives more oxygen, your body releases endorphins, which is a pain killer among other things!

There have been people who have laughed themselves well. Our organs take a natural jog during laughter, so indeed it does serve to heal and refresh the body, even relaxing us many times!

> *A merry heart doeth good like a medicine: but a broken spirit drieth the bones*—Proverbs 17:22.

I am full of the joy of the Lord and so many times my mouth is filled with laughter, and the joy of love and fun! I love to laugh and sometimes hunt things to laugh about. I love comedies, they are so relaxing and so enjoyable! I wanted to share some laughter with you so I decided to write some funny things. I hope you find them funny and laugh with me!

***

A little misunderstanding:
"Waiter, come here at once," the agitated diner called. "Can you explain why there is a footprint in the middle of my food?"
"Yes, sir, You ordered an omelet and told me to **step** on it."

***

In his Sunday morning sermon, a preacher recently announced that there are 726 different kinds of sin. Since that Sunday morning, he has been besieged with requests for the lists, mostly from people who are afraid that they are missing something.

***

A local priest and a pastor stood by the side of the road holding up a sign that read. "The end is near! Turn yourself around now before it is too late!" They planned to hold up the sign to each passing car.
"Leave us alone you religious nuts!" yelled the first driver as he sped by. From around the curve, they heard a big splash.
"Do you think." said one clergyman to the other, "we should just put up a sign that says "Bridge Out," instead?"

***

One evening a wife drew her husband's attention to the couple next door. She took him out on the porch so he could see what they were doing. Pointing across the yard, she said, "Do you see that couple? How devoted they are? He kisses her every time they meet. I notice that he often brings home **flowers or** dinner. Why don't you ever do that?"

"I would love to," replied the husband amiably and smoothly "but I don't know her well enough!"

Happy laughter and merry times to you!!!

WORDS

*Now therefore, listen to me, my children;
pay attention to the words of my mouth.*
Proverbs 7:24

WORDS, Yes, they can create or destroy…
unite or divide…they CAN…!
Words… the communication of the dominant kingdom
to the lower kingdom, animals,
two legged or four legged.
Words…the communication even to the plant kingdom
as well. (Jesus and fig tree).
Words are mental communication…
Words are spirit communications of the heart.

Many, many people live and die without ever really understanding the power of their words. Many times, We don't even grasp the power of God's Word—and cant—until it becomes rhema word to us. Let what I am saying become rhema word to you as you read, for it is truth.

I can believe you love me by the power of words! This is why we must also see action rather than believing just words. You can also cause me to doubt if you love me with just your words.

My mentor, Dr. Mike Murdock, teaches that God loved words so much He called Himself "The Word." The more you think about the fact that Jesus is called The Word—is The Word—the more you begin to realize the significance of words. Deep and powerful thoughts go with those words! Words are the most powerful thing on earth, except for prayer, but then prayer is composed of words!

Success in any endeavor whether business, relationships, raising children, or marriage depends on the words of our mouth. With words you fail in any area or succeed! Having this knowledge one would think that we would engage our mind...just hesitate for one minute...in order to avoid saying the wrong things. We do not, most of the time, whether we be the smartest one around or the wisest one around.

Only God can tame the tongue, and oh yes—He can! This is why man has said, "I am getting tired of eating crow!" This means he is being broken of speaking wrong words. The longer it takes you to learn to control your tongue the longer it will take you to become successful. Unfortunately some must lose great things in order to learn this power of words.

God gives us the knowledge and the wisdom so He can change us and our outcome by controlling our tongue. Those who will not control thoughts—their mind, will also not control their words. If we cannot control our words then our words and our lives are out of control and out of order! Expect that to happen because it will and does!

Much could be said about words. Men have built a life of dreams with words and torn them down with their words in one sentence. Wives and husbands have destroyed their dreams with just words, many times.

The sad part of words is that the results of them and the memory of them—no one has the ability to erase. Once they are out of the mouth, they are like tooth paste out of the tube, only a fool would think he can put it back the way it was! God warned us many times of our words. He said a lot about words. He described how we should talk, how, and what we think, our meditation becomes words.

David said, *Let the words of my mouth be acceptable to thee oh God.* He asked for God to let his meditation, his thoughts in other words, be acceptable. He understood out of his thoughts would come right or wrong words! *But let your yes, be yes, and your no be no. For whatever is more than these is from the evil one*!—Matthew 5: 37. A lot to think about!...

THINK!!! Do we need deliverance from what we are thinking? For what is in the heart proceeds right out of the mouth! You may mean what you said, but did you mean to do what your words did to that person, to that dream you have or now—had?

> We cannot always say what we want to…
> It's called consideration of others…
> with our words—our conversations!!!

DREAMS

Beautiful dreams are from God.
Sometimes, what we consider 'bad dreams' are warnings or alerts from God.

I believe that a dream is what issues forth from the heart that God places there in us. Sometimes dreams can be hidden. Just as it takes some inspiration for our faith to be lifted it also takes the right trigger, maybe a dream while sleeping, to cause a dream in our heart to become known or kindled into an action.

I am not talking about the ambitious dream of **building a** big business, a big home with all the beautiful things in it. I am talking about a dream, not an ambition.

A dream comes through the heart because it is a spiritual thing that comes from our God who is Spirit. I am talking about something called the dream that is bigger than you are and the reason is because it did come from God. I am talking about a dream that will have a need for God to pull it off. He is the one that placed it there and he is the one with all the puzzle pieces and all the correct moves and turns to get you there. It is what He created you to become very successful in doing.

I believe if we could really get very familiar with the desires of our hearts we would discover the dream for us that God placed there when He created us. I believe that is God's dream for us; to establish that desire in our lives. All we have to do is be obedient and let him lead us. We may not know today where all our obedience will lead us, but God does. I wonder if this is how someone has come to say just follow that dream for it leads to the rainbow at the end. Much has been said about that.

Obedience to God does lead us to our purpose, our dream for our life. We seldom ever will find the dream that comes true supernaturally without the help of God. When we find that dream, and begin to work on it, then we can safely say that the creator and the created have agreed!

Imagine the Creator of the universe designing your dream for you and then faithfully standing with you until it supernaturally happens as you just keep on loving the Dream Maker. His dream for you will always encompass His purpose for you. It's all about you and Him and His dream and your dream becoming one dream—

THE DREAM!!!

Have you found God? Are you faithful to meet with Him and seek His direction? If you have found God, and you have sought His direction and you have walked with Him…may I say—for sure—you will find that dream!!! God will take you to that dream or that "dream one!" God cannot lie!!! *Delight yourself in the Lord; and He shall give you the desires of your heart*!—Psalm 37:4.

With God it is never too late to start dreaming because 'the better" with God is always just ahead of you, in life and in death.

If you have found your dream, grab it with both hands. Hold on tight and never, never, never stop thanking God, for it is the reason for what He is going to do with you…and yours!!!

Hallelujah!!!

God is good!!!

Forever more He is good…there is no end to the goodness of God!!!

May God bless you in having your wildest dreams come true!!!

PLACE

For sure everyone is "some place!"

We have either arrived there by our words, our decisions, our health, our actions, reactions, birth, and even choices. One thing is certain, if we are walking together with our Father in obedience then we are at peace in the place we now occupy.

I tweeted today that when we are in the wrong place we are not effective, but will be affected by everything in and around that wrong place. It will all be wrong and with wrong outcomes until we let God correct it!

Everything is an exchange...what we have to do to find a place is make an exchange of something. When we exchange good for evil then we can be sure that in that place there will be much exchanging of evil instead of that which is good!

Nothing good is ever birthed in the wrong place...we may think so for a season but one day reality meets with deception and we see the light at last. Sometimes we must listen to the trusted voice even though we see no danger today. We must believe that God sends those trusted voices to spare us in our peaceful place and avoid sin in the defeated place.

There are many places! It can be a mental place, physical place, spiritual place, even an imaginary place. God spoke much of places. The verse is quoted, (especially by those who dislike prosperity teaching), that Jesus had no place to lay His head. This was not speaking of a physical home. This was meaning no place to hide from His calling, no place to hide from persecution or death. No real son of God has this place of rest where he can lay his head down. If man has such a place, he is not a son of God but a coward of fear, not faith. Fear is only a temporary bed of comfort. In 2 Corinthians 4:7-12, we see others who had no resting place.

In Jesus ministry and in our true ministry place, we have no place to run to from these things. The honor of God rest in the right place. Psalm 26. The right place is an even place, David told us so. We have no rough places to walk alone for God is walking before us making the path straight in that place. In the right place we are hidden from our enemies. God wants us to be completely devoted to Him for that is the only place the Holy Spirit will rest. Who will build that place for Him?

God's place is with you in your right place, and He said if you disobey He will return to His own place until you repent, Hosea 5:15. God will not stay with you in the wrong place and that is why everything in your life will be affected in an evil way.

The Jewish rulers foolishly thought that if they did not do away with Jesus then they would lose their place and nation! Yes read it! John 11:48. God even told us to leave room in our lives for those on whom He will take revenge for their evil ways! We don't have to do it in our right place. He will, and He said give me room in this place for that!

God's word also tells us…give no room to the devil. (He has a place to, but not in our lives!) There are dark places of evil and great places of the light of God. The more of God, the brighter the place! The right place leads us into pleasant places!!! Make the place you dwell the dwelling place of future generations, Psalm 90:1!

There is even a safe place for the person who, in spite of satan's attempt to stop them, will persevere to the doing of God's will, Revelation 12:6!

> Arise today and find your right place,
> and if you are in your right place,
> let your light shine bright in that place!!!

KINDNESS

Kind – Fit for use.
Kindness – Prone to love, Virtuous, Cherishing, Good.

True kindness is not that which is taught in kindergarten, or in the "manners class." Many have been fooled by thinking that type of **education** of kindness in a person was indicative of their true kindness. There are many who have been taught, even raised to be kind, but they are not really a kind person in their heart.

Real kindness is birthed from a pure heart of love. Real kindness is the manifestation of the love of God in our words, in our thoughts, in our lives and in the way we live. Kindness is a lifestyle. It is walking softly through this world in the hearts and lives of those around us.

If you are a thoughtful person, you will be a kind person. Thoughtfulness is the demonstration of love for others feelings, and consideration of their place and life. People who are kind are loving people, with a loving mind towards others. If you are un-thoughtful, you are not a kind person.

Jesus is our kindness. It is Christ in us the hope of glory that births kindness in us. There are no depths to kindness, you are either a kind person or you are not. There is no "in between." If we just go through life making decisions, doing like we please—only considering ourselves—then there is no kindness in us, even if we are not speaking unkind words.

We are not islands, so every choice we make, everything we do, whether spoken or not tells others of our kindness, and thoughtfulness or it does not. We have an instruction from God: *Be ye kind to one another,* Ephesians 4:32.

Some people just act, speak—live—and never think of the thoughts and feelings of others! This is a very unkind person. They have not developed the fruit of the Spirit in their lives. When the love of God is shed abroad in our lives, then we will become very kind to all peoples, even our enemies and those who would oppose us.

One of the descriptions of love in the Word of God is that "love is kind". Do you realize that if we are not speaking words of faith they are not kind words? Words that are kind are positive words, words of life for another and that is kindness. Negative words contain death, not kindness, life, or love.

You see if we speak like with a tongue of an angel and do not speak in love then our sound is nothing but as a clanging cymbal, (1 Corinthians 13:1) which is only a noise, bringing forth nothing. If a person is full of the love of God their kindness will be consistent and with expressions in many ways.

There is absolutely no kindness in evil, none! Kindness requires no planning. It is always flowing from the loving heart. There is no end to kindness for there is no end of the love of God. In the heart of a true servant there will be found great kindness. Our God is the abundance of kindness! David said in Psalms 31 that God had shown him marvelous kindness.

The tongue of the Proverbs 31 woman is that of kindness when she opens her mouth. Most, even Christian women, cannot even get to that part! Unkind words and actions grieve the Holy Spirit for He is love. My mentor, Dr. Mike Murdock, has a wisdom key that goes like this: "People don't always remember what you say–they always remember how they felt when you said it."

> *But in all things approving ourselves as the ministers of God, in much patience...by pureness, by knowledge, by longsuffering, by kindness, by the Holy Ghost, by love unfeigned*, 2 Corinthians 6:4,6.

Father, help us to open our mouths always in kindness,
edifying others, not destroying others,
so that our words are acceptable in Thy sight,
Oh Lord, my strength, and my redeemer,
in Christ Jesus' name.
Amen.

FORERUNNER

One who comes in advance
to a place where the rest are to follow.

The greatest example and the open and revealed message of the forerunner today: John the Baptist! The kingdom of God is at hand! The way must be prepared just like we do for a king or a president.

This is the King of Kings and Lord of Lords!!!

In fact, though John the Baptist was indeed the forerunner that came before the Lord calling everyone to repentance and making straight the way of the Lord, the only time the word "forerunner" is used in the King James version is in Hebrews 6:20. Here it is talking about Jesus being the forerunner for us, having entered in behind the veil as High Priest.

He is coming back for His bride, (I use the singular for when we are in one accord we will be one: the bride, who is living in holiness and the wisdom of God.) He came the first time fulfilling the words of the forerunner prophets. He came the first time with the forerunners being angels that heralded His coming into this world. His return will be foreshadowed this time as well by His messengers with the message of a forerunner. They will be:

> *The voice of one crying in the wilderness: prepare the way of the Lord; Make straight in the desert a highway for our God. Every valley shall be exalted and every mountain and hill brought low; the crooked places shall be made straight and the rough places smooth; the glory of the Lord shall be revealed and all flesh shall see it together; for the mouth of the Lord has spoken*—Isaiah 40:3-5.

We shall see the glory of God on these forerunners who are living a holy life and declaring Holiness, Holiness, Holiness! Those of us who are here now are teaching those younger ones who are carrying the anointing. For all shall see this great glory of our God!

The best display of the glory of God is His emotions in His Bride. Joy, oh joy!!! The world will see it just as they saw the foolish ones and the wise virgins. All flesh shall see it!

There is always great persecution for the person who has a message that requires change and where religious spirits rest. There are forerunners today, for every 2000 years God sends a deliverer for his people. The first one was Moses, the second one was Jesus and the third one is the bride of Christ, the "now" forerunner!

This is what we are doing today as forerunners! We are bringing deliverance today to those in poverty, for the Bride of Christ is not in poverty in finances, health or life! The anointings now are so strong some think they are going to die if they don't teach or preach or have big healing meetings. These leaders with holiness in heart are forerunners who are ministering to Christians to teach, and deliver them for the desire of God's heart and rulership in His kingdom.

Forerunner, take His word and it will come alive with that anointing, for the spirit of the living God is on you, the forerunner, to make the way holy for the King to reign as the head of and on the body of Christ. There must be the forerunners to accomplish this. Don't wait for the position, don't wait for the great meeting, start where you are proclaiming the truths of the living God!!!

In Acts, read what it says about the refreshing time that must come...no one is refreshed unless they are restored and blessed!!! Healing and wholeness for the total man; the bride. This is what the loving God desires for His bride today. Now we are seeing all things uncovered that are hidden for there cannot be justice or healing for things that are hidden.

Our light shines brighter and brighter as Isaiah said it would as we live out the holiness of our God in our everyday life and proclaim it where ever we go!!! One requirement is Holiness of God in the pure heart!

The Kingdom of God is at hand!
No one faint of heart will ever be a forerunner for our King!!
Repent! Repent! Repent!

LOVE

...*The Greatest Is LOVE*
I Corinthians 13:13

Can't stop it!

Can't hide it!

Can't describe it!

Can't end it!

Can't change it!

Can't buy it!

Can't ignore it!

Can't resist it!

Can't see it!

Can't control it!

Can't box it!

Can't Conquer it!

Can't forget it!

Can't weigh it!

Can't measure it!

Can't destroy it!

Can't subtract from it!

Can't kill it!!!

FORCE!!!

But…it can do many things.

We can do many things with it, for it,

because of it,

and unto it!!!

For God is love!!!

He who does not love does not know God for God is love.
1 John 4:8.

Love is life!!!

Life is love!!!

Got love today….or milk?

RESTITUTION

Restore/Make Complete

Restitution is a word that very, very few ministers or evangelist ever talk about. Jesus talked about it and told us to do this...make restitution. If we stole something, it must be returned and if not possible, then something of the same kind and thing should be returned! Actually, excellence would call for a better return than what was stolen.

When we are the cause of someone losing something, then we should be the reason if at all possible that "thing" returns to their life. We can damage something and it needs to be replaced if we are the one responsible for the damage.

We do not have to damage someone with or in a physical thing, it can be a word. It can destroy them, their dreams and maybe their hope for a future. If we have done this then we need to make restitution! We need to make it right! We don't have to steal to take from a person, we can cause them to be wounded in their spirit with our words and this has subtracted from them and left them with less.

We need to apologize and realize that we can steal with our words, very much so!!!

2 Corinthians 7:10 tells us that, *Godly sorrow produces repentance leading to salvation....*

When we receive Jesus into our heart, His love comes into our heart and we start feeling bad when we see the truth of what we have done in our sins. We are very sorry we hurt that person, took from that person, stole from that person. We must make it as right as we can for that which is in our **power** to correct and make restitution.

When we are truly repentant we are truly honest about what God shows us about our lives and others we have oppressed or done wrong. When we repent and make restitution it is maybe the best way to prove repentance has happened to us and that we are changed. It is also one of the best ways to start restoring credibility and integrity within oneself. When we apologize, or return things and make things right, then others not only see our change, they see a clear picture of salvation and they see the goodness of our God.

When we walk in this kind of holiness and His goodness becomes witnessed in our lives we will see His glory there as well...for where we see the goodness of God we also see His glory. Many have been led to the Lord because someone made restitution, someone apologized, someone walked in truth!!!

Restitution is proof you are truly sorry and you have changed. Anyone is touched when they see this kind of honesty in another person, especially if they have been hurting because of our sins. One of the requirements Jesus told the man in His word was return what you have stolen! Does no one ever read Exodus 22 now days? Have we forgotten what God said about restitution.

I always say that there are three things that some Christians find hard to utter from their lips. It is these words:
- I sinned.
- I am sorry.
- Please forgive me!

That is as far as some will go and many, many have never said these words or even asked:
- Was I wrong?
- Do I need to ask forgiveness?

For sure these people will not seek to make restitution. God and His holiness demand it. Very few people will ever apologize...and even fewer will make restitution their goal. Read all of Exodus 22! Read what God's word says! *But if, in fact, it is stolen from him, he shall make restitution to the owner of it*—Exodus 22:12.

This is plain and clear, if we took it, then we must replace it, better than before!

What have you never returned and told the truth about....

What?

Hebrew Meaning:
Restitution—To be in a covenant of peace!

FORGIVENESS
THE ROAD TO A HAPPY LIFE

Release from bondage or prison.
Remission of the penalty

Forgiveness is the act of understanding the one who, without the love of our Father in their heart, acted or said something that was not right. Understanding knows that they are not realizing what they are doing. True forgiveness does not demand restitution!

Forgiveness understands the lack of the Fathers love in someone's life. Anything that births the need for one to forgive is not a right thing, a good thing, but sin. If we walk in the light as He is in the light, (the truth), then we can love without sinfully offending.

When we forgive we give up all claim, all demand for payment and all demands of restitution. The one offending may feel these needs, but forgiveness does not require it. Forgiveness understands there are those who are incapable of feelings and thoughtfulness without the love of our Father in their heart. We have really put ourselves upon the throne when we cannot forgive.

Jesus, our example, forgave a man at the cross who had lived his whole life against Him and His will. He required nothing except the man recognize He was Lord and that he was a sinner. If Christ sits on the throne of our heart then He is our forgiveness even when we cannot find it in our self to forgive. It is not us who lives, but Christ who lives in us!

Doctors, health officials, ministers, and God know that any unforgiveness we may hold brings disease and death just like every other sin. Paul prayed that the church at Philippi would be sincere and without offense...for that is the root of unforgiveness (offense—off and ended).

If we do not forgive then Jesus cannot forgive our sins. He forgives all our iniquities, even healing all our diseases! (Psalm 103).

We always need to ask forgiveness to make it real
and we need to forgive to make it right.

Sometimes we have to not bother the person who is not receptive to our asking forgiveness, but forgive them in our heart. Wisdom says this is the protocol in that case. Forgiveness is the first step of restoration of a broken relationship due to offense.

When we forgive we set ourselves free. It is the one place where we can choose to set ourselves free when we forgive another. To the extent of our forgiveness will be the measure of the extent of our happiness. *The discretion of a man makes him slow to anger, and his glory is to overlook a transgression*—Proverbs 19:11.

- Have you asked forgiveness from those you did not treat right, did not speak to in love?

- Have you developed a lifestyle of never taking offense because the love of the Father dwells within you today?

- Have you told Jesus He is your forgiveness when you could not forgive and you saw it was not within you to forgive?

Talk to God today and ask Him to give you the kind of love that may know some hurt but will not take offense. If you will, you are going to see you are well on your road to a lifestyle of less regrets and more happiness!!!

Forgiveness, the road to happiness!!!

THE INTERCESSOR

> One who intervenes
> on behalf of truth and right.

I could write a lot about the intercessor and intercession. Much has been written about it; many books. Today, let's just concentrate on the intercessor!

Who is an intercessor you may ask.

An intercessor is one who has a calling, just like any other ministry is a calling. It is greatly misunderstood and it is not honored as God would have it be honored. The first and foremost requirement for God to bless a person with the calling of intercessor is for that person to be a man or woman of God that loves people. That person must want the will of God for others more than he wants to become a great success himself. He must love people, for at the call of God on any day, any hour he must drop what he is doing and submit to that call by praying for others.

He is the one who takes the needs of others to our Father. He loves to do it for he loves to pray. The one who makes prayer a first and foremost thing in his life is the one who will receive the call to come deeper..., "Come to be my intercessor," says God to him.

The intercessor stands in the gap, between earth and the throne of God. A true intercessor prays under an open heaven. All intercession is prayer, but not all prayer is intercession. God listens to and communes often with a true intercessor. God can do nothing on this earth unless we ask Him to, for Jesus gave us all that authority when He left the earth. He said you do not have because you do not ask.

The intercessor is asking. Because of his willing heart towards God, and his love for others, he is asking in the spirit for God wants to do great things. God must have someone to ask! He knew He needed someone willing to seek His face at the expense of leaving his own success on the table. I know of no true intercessor that God does not bless with the greatest communication between heaven and earth.

Sometimes the call from the earth to God is so deep, so great, it becomes a ministry of intercession through tears. When you measure the success of the intercessor with worldly goods, you are measuring with man's yardstick instead of God's yardstick of measurement. It will one day shock many when they see all that happened to them and their great blessings that only came because someone hidden away in a dark closet, maybe under the prayer shawl, an intercessor, stood on their knees in the gap for them before God.

As long as there is one who is called and can beseech the name of Jesus for others, there will be change and answers. Jacob prayed under an open heaven, the ladder was his intercession, answers by angels were coming down from heaven to him and angels were carrying his prayers into heaven.

During World War Two a group of soldiers were sent

from a small town in Texas. There were several intercessors who met each day and prayed for them. When the war was over they returned home without a scratch. Intercession makes a difference.

Thank God one day God will rule this world, but He is not ruling this world today! The true intercessor is ruling this world today by intercession and asking God to rule and reign. The intercessor argues man's case before a holy and righteous God.

Job, in Chapter 9, recognized the need for an intercessor to plead his case.

In Isaiah 59:16 we see that when God found no intercessor He sent Jesus. This is why we should honor true intercessors. They are of significance and great importance to the plans of God. He wishes none to perish!!!

Paul prayed for the Colossians and did not stop. Paul travailed for the church in Galatia. We must be willing to be called to intercession!

If I find in Sodom fifty righteous within the city, then I will spare the place for THIER sakes, Genesis 18:26.

Intercessor, you may not see it today, but ... in heaven will you receive the deserving honor for all that you saved from destruction!

Keep praying!!!

FRIENDSHIP

*A friend loveth at all times,
and a brother is born for adversity.*
Proverbs 17:17

- A friend is our true wealth.
- A friend is one who knows us—our faults and all—and loves us anyway!
- A friend is a treasure God gives us, a great gift that needs to be appreciated and that friendship always honored.
- A true friend will tell us the truth even at the cost of the friendship, but in words tied together with love and prayer. He is trustworthy and forever faithful even at keeping confidentialities.
- A friend is someone well known to us, who shares intimate thoughts and feelings.

We can never confuse an acquaintance as being a friend.

- Friends walk together in harmony, in accord, in understanding and rapport.
- A friend is our alley who will rise to our side in a cause to fight.

- A friend **supports** us and shares our dream of becoming what it is in our heart to do or be. He is a comrade and companion day in and day out. He will be our advocate. He likes us first and as the friendship grows, begins to love us.
- He will stand up for us and "go to bat" for us with loyalty, even at his own cost. He knows our interest, and always seeks our best interest in all situations.
- A true friend will not forsake us, but in times of trouble he will encourage us and stay with us…walking it out with us!

There will be few who will be there with us without any questions when we need them, these are the gems, the ones who give sparkle to our lives and greater meanings to all we are and do!

If you have a Godmate, then you are twice blessed for God has given you a great mate who is also your very best friend on this earth!

Make yourself memorable by being a best friend to someone today for the rest of their life—someone you like—someone you have grown to love, and never stop loving them, being there for them!!!

> "When God wants to bless you,
> He brings a person into your life!!!"
> Dr. Mike Murdock

GRATITUDE

On occasion, but not real often,
we meet a person of great gratitude.

When we see this quality of pleasantness in a person then we can know this person of great gratitude has known great and heartfelt losses in his or her life. We can know this for they have learned to cherish the precious and show pleasantness of gratitude for all things that come their way. They have indeed suffered from loses and most times, not from their own wrong doing. They are well acquainted with grief in their life that has come by emotional and sometimes physical losses.

I believe that there is no such thing as excess in gratitude, when demonstrated properly. I think it may be true that gratitude is the essence of good mental health and the acknowledgment of God and His life in the person. A person who is filled with the love of God seems to always turn to gratitude in the event of a loss while the rebel will turn to bitterness many, many times.

I read a book once that was about why bad things make some people better and some people bitter. I think when a person is full of the love of God, loss does not turn to bitterness. This person seems to always remember there is one who they have not lost: Jesus! They recognize with great gratitude He is the only one who will never leave them, or ever let them go.

Expressed feelings in words or in actions, can demonstrate thankfulness—gratitude. People who are full of gratitude create warm feelings towards others of being appreciated. There has even been research that shows that the one who is focused in a thanksgiving posture is one whose happiness seems to increase. Most all grateful people are happy people who are forever riding above their circumstances!

Gratitude is an attitude that should never leave us, it will cause depression to run and hide, and we can keep depression at bay all our lives with thankfulness in our hearts for everything!!! Do you not suppose maybe Paul knew this and that is why he said, *Giving thanks ALWAYS for ALL things unto God and the Father in the name of our Lord Jesus Christ.*

How many times have you been thankful in the name of Jesus Christ? This is the will of God, so we are either in the will of God here with our gratitude or we are in disobedience to His will. *In EVERY THING give thanks; for this is the will of God in Christ Jesus concerning* you—1 Thessalonians 5:18.

In my opinion that is the verse that keeps depression at a great distance from us. If you are depressed you may not have been thanking God for all things He has gifted you with and for those He sent into your life who are and have been a blessing to you.

Gratitude is simply expressing pleasure for something that has been done or given.

It is expressing kindness for that which has been received. It's that simple! God even told us to come into his presence with thanksgiving, to be thankful for all things, even in 1 Timothy 2:1, He says to be thankful for all men!

Could there be something there about all men that we keep overlooking? It may be because all men are created in the image of God, saint or sinner. I think maybe it is because we must recognize—whether we like it or not—everyone who comes into our lives is either teaching us something or we are teaching them something!

Let us show kindness in thanksgiving for those things and those people who have blessed us in sweet and wonderful ways!!!

Even thank God for those who demonstrate these pleasant feelings through their thanksgiving to us!!!

SECURITY

Everyone wants it!
Some seek it.
Some think they have it!

There is very little need for an explanation of what exactly this word means, but I believe there may be a need to talk about it so there is no misunderstanding of it.

Our words and actions can even make another feel great feelings of "no security" in a relationship, whether it be a loved one or a member of our family. One more reason for choosing words rather than using words.

Love for others should cause us to really stop and think about what we do, what we say, how we say it and to whom we say it. If we do not feel freedom from theft, danger, care, or fear, then we will start having feelings of insecurity.

In order to stop feelings of not being secure, it will require someone, or something, or a plan that we can trust in.

We need to feel secure in our salvation; and that we are safe in believing that we are going to heaven and not hell when we exit this earth. The only way we can be sure of this is that we have received Jesus as our personal savior and we walk in obedience to His word.

Security can make us feel as if we are loved, and wanted, safe—even to the extent of making us feel like we are safe in the place where we exist, physically or in the spirit.

- Children can hear words that make them feel secure in their home and in their family life.
- A wife needs to feel security in her relationship with her husband.
- A Father needs to feel security in his place of honor as the head of the family.
- A pastor needs to feel security in what he does as a shepherd of his flock.

Any time we do not feel security it will play out in some form, emotionally, physically, or even spiritually. True security is the seed for feeling freedom from care, anxiety, doubt. The voice, the plan, and the words that bring security must contain trustworthiness because these things must be believable in order to bring the security that is needed.

We must first trust in God before we will ever find true security for in man and in this world there is no security. No amount of money can buy it. We have recently, in our economy and in the world, seen how little security there actually is without God.

This is the significance of teaching others and family about God for He is our security in all things at all times. He is the one that makes us feel safe, protected and defended with His love and His word for us.

David said others can trust in many things, even in horses and chariots, but he will believe in our God. The reason David said this is because the Israelites did not fight with chariots and horses, because God wanted them to see that He was their security for victory! The enemy always had what should have made the Israelites feel insecure, but David and his warriors were secure with our God.

The word tells us to, *Trust in the Lord with all thine heart; and lean not unto thine own understanding. In all they ways acknowledge Him and He will direct thy paths.* Proverbs 3:5-6. Only a trust in God, His plan, and the things of God can bring us security that we need to have in order to live securely. That requirement is trust in God completely.

"Trust God; love men." Dr. Mike Murdock.

A trustworthy voice can bring rest, relieve anxiety, and cause us to experience security!

There is no greater place of security than the heart of our Father!

THE GODMATE

And the rib, which the LORD God had taken from man, made He a woman, and brought her unto the man.
Genesis 2:22

Most of the singles get excited when they hear the word, Godmate. Some refer to that "right one" as the soul mate. I know that God can make a relationship so divine it will be better than any soul mate, but will be His Godmate for you.

No one seems to ever talk too much about this, but it should be talked about and the three necessary ingredients to joining up with that Godmate should be explored for our God is a God of order and He has His order in His divine relationship as well.

<u>The first step is the spiritual step</u>. This is honoring God's laws again. We never want to link ourselves with those who are not walking with our God, not in business or pleasure of friendships. It will not take too long in actions and reactions and studying this person and learning from their life, where they are in their walk with Christ. When we have determined they are of the same spiritual beliefs and levels as ourselves, then we become more interested and

this person begins to take shape in our thoughts as an individual rather than just someone in the group.

Perhaps by this time God may even have spoken to both, or one, or the other to let them know, "This is my Godmate." Do not go by feelings here. You must know the voice of the Holy Spirit on this. It should be confirmed out of the mouth of not less than two or three witnesses when God speaks to you and tells you who the Godmate is.

He will ALWAYS confirm His word. He promised us this. These are people who know nothing of what God has spoken to you. If you have told them, then they are not confirming, they are just agreeing with what you are just merely thinking.

The second step is becoming what is known in the world as a "couple," or boyfriend and girlfriend. This is why the first step is so important, because this is when you get involved emotionally and with your heart. Both must be feeling the same things throughout this time or it will never get to the next and most serious step.

This is when you get to know and understand what makes this person who they are and the deeper things of their lives. You find out here how they feel about things and hopefully most all things of interest are shared interest. Similar interest and teachings throughout the two different lives began to merge into one.

Somewhere in this place we begin to know not only that we love this person, but that we want to spend the rest of our lives with them. We stop thinking of today and start thinking of tomorrows and building dreams together. After much prayer, and agreement during this time we know we feel safe, we know we feel secure, but most of all we know it is of God and it is not a man's plan. It is at this time that the man begins to take the lead.

We then step into the most serious time of all. We now

separate ourselves more and more from our past friends of the opposite sex. We can no longer be socializing with those of the opposite sex for now we have involved another life and heart in our life and heart. We forsake all others for now it is the man who ask this woman to be his wife. He is serious about spending the rest of his life with her and she is saying, "Yes," and he begins building his whole life around her and their dreams together.

Here they plan futures together, dream together, discuss financial issues and all they would like to see happen. They plan their wedding and set the date. This is a very serious time.

At this point in time all others must be forsaken for there is only room for these two to become one.

In the Word dating is not even discussed. In the Word of God the Holy Spirit directs all of the relationships of marriage that God tells us about. God still does this today. God can give you a divine relationship just like He did when He told Joseph he would wed Mary. God brought Esther to the king, and Ruth to Boaz. God gave Jacob his wife and the evil one tried to steal her, but he continued believing what God said. God brought Isaac's wife to him.

These are divine relationships that God has already foreordained and gave His approval for each step man must go through. He is still doing this today.

If you pray over and over again for God to give you a mate, you will think every man or woman you see is the one. You will become greatly deceived and perhaps enter a tragic relationship.

On the other hand, when you begin to think you would like to have a mate, tell God how you feel and ask Him to send the perfect one, the Godmate for you, then leave it up to Him!!! Ask Him to give you the wisdom to recognize that Godmate. They will definitely be a discovery and you will fit together like a hand in a glove.

GODMATES!

In that wonderful discovery you will find out that God knows you better than you know yourself! That Godmate…they will be better to you than you would be to yourself!!!

> *Therefore a man shall leave his father and mother*
> *and be joined to his wife*
> *and they shall become one flesh.*
> Genesis 2:24.

TIMING

I tweeted today,
"There is a time to speak and a time to be quiet,
and happy is the man whose wife discerns this!

Pure and simple—timing is thoughtfulness.

A person who is thinking of what he needs to say and do will also think about when to do this. He will consider his audience…be it 1 or 1,000. That thoughtful person will consider other persons' timing as well, and where they are in their timing—in their present focus!

Women have, at times, been accused of not always having correct timing. That may be true, I have thought a lot about that and I do have some thoughts on that as well. Perhaps it is because women are driven so much by emotions, and I have said before, that anxiety can cause loss of proper protocol.

Timing has a lot to do with the proper protocol and if I were going to put timing under a header, I am sure that is where I would put it. It just has so much to do with protocol. There is a time that is considered proper timing for anyone who wears a hat! That is one timing for sure that falls under protocol.

Great thoughts, never to be had again, broken by improper timing have been lost many times. Writers and thinkers are probably the ones most sensitive to proper timing of others.

There are many things to think about when you are deciding if this is the proper time for this. This is something that must be learned. We must consider many things when deciding from the actual time of day down to, is this a sensitive matter; too sensitive for right now?

Thoughtfulness, again, rules when proper timing is chosen! The Word of God has a long scripture about timing:

> *To everything there is a season, and a time to every purpose under the heaven: A time to be born, and a time to die; a time to plant, and a time to pluck up that which is planted; A time to kill, and a time to heal; a time to laugh; a time to mourn, and a time to dance; a time to cast away stones, and a time to gather stones together; a time to embrace, and a time to refrain from embracing; a time to get and a time to lose; a time to keep and a time to cast away; a time to rend, and a time to sew; a time to keep silence, and a time to speak; a time to love; and a time to hate; a time for war, and a time for peace.*
> Ecclesiastes 3:1-8.

My mentor, Dr. Mike Murdock says that "Doing the right thing at the wrong time becomes the wrong thing!"

So we see timing is of great significance! Timing must always be considered, no matter the act, no matter the word, it must be considered. If we move too quickly without giving time to think, then we will reap the consequences of the lack of thoughtfulness, and our timing will be poor!

A time for everything…wow…that is enough to think about for a long while!

Perfect timing—wouldn't that be wonderful?

Father, I ask You to look down on our frailties today,
and those places wherein we fall short
many times in our lives by moving ahead,
speaking ahead of the Holy Spirit.
Teach us, Father, more about thoughtfulness,
consideration, and love for others' timing
so that our timing becomes more perfected each day!
In Christ Jesus name we ask.
Amen

A RESTING PLACE?

*This is the resting place where I shall dwell;
for I have desired it.*
Psalm 132:14

Have you found that resting place in the Lord where you have relaxed in the trust you have in our Almighty God?

There are many places we think of when we think of resting place. The Lord said in His word that not everyone will find this place. When Jesus walked the earth He said He had no place to lay His head, unlike the birds even, that have their nests. He did not mean He did not have a home or a bed. He meant that He could not rest in this world for He had an assignment He had to fulfill.

He knew we cannot sleep and rest when we are in the enemy's camp. We cannot rest in that place. We must be always on guard, always knowing this is not our home, not the place to lay down and sleep or the enemy will take over our soul. No place to rest. That is a place that we cannot find rest.

There are places that David said God could find rest.

It is when the Holy Spirit finds a temple, that is completely sold out to God and then He finds the place where He can rest. It becomes that person who is carrying the presence of our God!

Another place of rest is when the sinner makes peace with our God and he finds rest from sin, guilt and shame. He finds a peaceful resting place in forgiveness. David so loved God! He said, *Surely I will not come into the tabernacle of my house, nor go up into my bed; I will not give sleep to mine eyes or slumber to my mine eyelids, Until I find out a place for the Lord, an habitation for the Mighty God of* Jacob—Psalm 132:3-5. He was talking about the presence of God for it was only there that he knew that God would rest.

Psalm 132:8 says, *Arise, Oh Lord into Thy rest, Thou, and the ark of Thy strength.* The ark is the presence of God. Arise was the ancient word meaning to stand up/forth with purpose, such as for moving the ark, Numbers 10:35-36. The ark represents the dwelling place or presence of God. Find His presence, the ark, and that is where He dwells! Are you the ark that God is finding rest in today? Have you created a resting place for our Master, Adoni?

There are resting places from physical labor, after battling, even after solving a problem or finding the end of a troublesome issue! There is rest upon discovering our assignment on this earth. There is a peace and rest that comes from knowing we are in the center of God's will and living in obedience to Him and His word. There is rest in finding a Godmate after lonely days are at last over. There are resting places in the shade of the life of someone great who brings us refreshing times and words.

An absence of motion contains peace, sweet peace; a resting place. We find rest from anything that tires, troubles, disturbs, or pains. This is why the secret place, where we always can find the presence of God is so refreshing. It is a place of rest for there is where we find our real home that we hesitate to even leave, don't want to leave, for it is the harbor, our home, for our heart on this earth. The more time we spend in that resting place the greater our peace.

The presence of God: our resting place! That is where God finds His place to rest too! It is our heart, His temple, that is in love with Him and He finds peace there and there He finds His dwelling place, His resting place is in our heart! *This is my resting place forever; here I will dwell for I have desired it! For the Lord has chosen Zion, He has desired it for His dwelling place*—Psalm 132:13-14! Zion, the holiness of God!!!

We have a resting place in the heart of the King of Kings!!!

SELF EFFACEMENT

…many that are first shall be last; and the last shall be first.
Matthew 19:30

Self-effacement. Some just have to be first. We have to be seen, we have to be heard and if we are not then someone must be sinning! What an attitude, you might say. But oh how true it is of so many.

The servant is the one who is seldom awarded, seldom recognized, but God said he is first! The least being the first. There are very few who, through an act of their own, or a habit of their own, modestly keep themselves in the background. It takes a greater strength—a great person, to sit quietly and let God be the one who promotes, rather than to have front and center from man.

Some have become offended when they got "scratched" from a plan. Some have been offended when they were not recognized or noticed or, believe it or not, because someone did not smile at them. I believe God puts His very beloved one in a hidden place, an inconspicuous place to test so that we can be tried and come out as pure gold.

A bad attitude because we are not recognized, not rewarded, not the center of attention is proof there is still work that the Holy Spirit needs to do in our life. This test is sometimes the qualifier for a life that will become a public life, a life God will put on display. For His plan, God wants to make sure that the foundation is of Him and not man.

When we have the attitude that we can "get up there" and do a better job, we are entertaining evil spirits. God said there was no greater man than John the Baptist, but yet, when He allowed him to be killed, He said Blessed is he who is not offended! We don't really understand all things about God and His promotions. We must keep our posture as a servant of God and not look to man to promote us, or even be given our raises on our paychecks.

John (the apostle) quoted John the Baptist in John 3:30, *He, (meaning Jesus), must increase and I must decrease*. This is a decrease, a dying of our flesh so that we can walk in love, in the spirit of the Living God and be transformed in our minds; in our lives—then we can be truly self-effacing. Only then with a servants heart and recognizing it is God we serve. He is the one who promotes, we do not promote ourselves. It will be then, with an attitude of great love, that we will see God's promotion in our lives!

Rest assured we will be rewarded for our servant-hood!!! Matthew 23:12 tells us that, *whoever exalts himself will be humbled and he who humbles himself will be exalted*. Don't try to make anything happen, trust God to make it happen and He will!!!

God knows what He is doing, and He was the one who made those plans for you!

Submit to the Holy Spirit.
He will keep you in His perfect timing!!!

CONTENTMENT

The place of greatest contentment on earth is
in obedience to our Fathers will.

When we discover the plan and the dream God Himself has for our lives we find great contentment!!! We are satisfied mentally and emotionally for God is the creator and He knows us—what we need in things and who the person or persons are who will be content with us and us with them. Each will know fulfillment and contentment!

With God we do not even need to be discontent physically, for He will satisfy us with things we did not know we even needed because He knows us better than we know ourselves. He knows that perfect geographical area, that perfect home, office, etc., that person, He made just for us!!!

He designed us and knows what it will take to also bring us great contentment in our everyday life and walk with Him. He does this in relationships. He knows what will make us happy! He knows exactly what will bring us contentment, satisfaction, and remove all desires for anyone else, all else for He has so fulfilled us.

When we peacefully receive and accept that calling, that destiny that God had for us all along, then the next thing that follows is great contentment. We know we had questions but God is answering all of them as we questioned the things even about ourselves that He created in us. Our needs, the things that will make us complete, also are the things that bring us fulfillment and great contentment.

Paul said in 1 Timothy 6:6: *Godliness with contentment is great gain*! GREAT GAIN, think of that for a minute. When the word of God says "Great," imagine how gigantic a measurement that must be!!!

There is no ease of mind, no contentment for the person acting or living outside of the will and plan God has for their life. The fool is the one who thinks he can improve on what God has given him. Only a fool walks away from what God has said, what He has instructed us to do. A fool may appear to be happy, but soon that disappears and discontentment begins in his life.

Everything that is not of God in our lives will bring discontentment sooner or later. Never forget that! Never!

When we cannot find this place of contentment we will keep looking until we find God and when we find God and His plan, then all searching stops for He has erased the needs and made us satisfied in this thing He has given us!!! Oh what a grace!!! There is no contentment like knowing satisfaction in God.

When we find that contentment we can focus better than we ever have, do things we never could do, create like we never could, achieve more than we ever could! Now our minds are no longer splintered in different directions, but focused only on that which God called us to do and be—at last!!! All discontentment, wondering, searching, and even sometimes doubt are now over forever!!! How beautiful is our God.....after all!!!!!

There is contentment when we become what God planned for us from the foundation of the earth. Greater than this is knowing that God had a dream Himself—for us!!! It's not just our dream and what we wanted, but what God Himself dreamed for us!!! What great contentment and joy to know we are living God's dream for us...fulfilling our own dream for ourselves and living in perfect contentment in His will!!!

Praise the Lord!!!
God is good!!!
Lord, You make me very happy!!!

MERCY

Goodness—Kindness--Faithfulness

I know I am going somewhere today where angels might fear to tread. I do it with humbleness before my God for direction of my thoughts and the words of my pen. Much, much could be said about mercy, that which has been shown to us, that which we have and do show towards others, and then, of course, God's mercy to us and to others.

First of all my belief is that mercy is more kindness extended than justice requires. When kindness far outweighs the justice then it has become misplaced mercy, extended to someone undeserving. When a person continues to accept our mercy and kindness when they know in their heart they do not deserve it, then it is time to start questioning our mercy—or is it misplaced mercy?

Mercy is kindness that is beyond what can be claimed or expected. Mercy is something that ALL should be thankful for, it is indeed one of God's richest gifts to us. It seems to me that God shows mercy according to the motive of the person, or motives whichever the case may be.

Many times, mercy does not change a situation, nor does it always change the person who receives it. So we could say there is not much change included in mercy, even though we may secretly be hoping so.

There are some who have lived on misplaced mercy most of their lives from others. There are some who do not get in need, too much, for mercy for they live very godly lives after God showed them great mercy and saved them. Mercy is the greatest measure of small or large kindnesses that I believe exists on this earth.

If we are merciful, we will obtain mercy when we are in need of it, says the word of God. If a person has lost divine favor and purpose for being in our life, when we discover it, then continue to show mercy, it has then become misplaced mercy.

In almost every life there comes a time when God, Himself, cuts off His mercy. Remember God sees the motive, the plot in the heart of a person where man cannot, and He seems to deal with them accordingly.

Abraham was shown mercy when he lied, even from our God who said, "I hate Liars." He did not say, I hate lying, He said I hate a liar. When Ananias and Sapphira lied, they were struck down because they not only lied but did it in the house of God, in the presence of God and His glory, and to a man of God. Peter said they actually agreed together to lie to the Holy Spirit. He said they had lied, not to men, but to God, so when we lie to a man of God, we have lied to God as well.

The wrong motive behind an act or a word directed towards or concerning the heart of a man of God does not seem to be that which God shows His mercy towards! When a person loses favor with a man of God or a righteous person, they have also at that moment lost favor with God. It is then time to end our mercy also, for mercy is the proof that there is still favor with God.

The time of mercy does stop. Anything beyond this point does not seem to me to line up with the knowledge of God that I have learned. Again, when Korah and others, came up against the man of God the earth swallowed them up and some were struck with leprosy. God will not tolerate that which negatively affects a man of God, a son of God.

The disregard of God's will as revealed in the law is not merely to break an isolated rule; it is to rebel against God, Himself. We are not to reward rebels. The very reason things happen to those who have shown no honor or mercy to a man of God, and others, will, in their time of judgment receive no mercy in judgment from God.

When we realize these things have been done, the time for our mercy has come to an end. We can remain kind without involving mercy or entertaining that person in our lives. "It is law to the proud and grace to the humble" (Dr. Mike Smalley).

So when we show mercy, it is not according to our standards and what makes us feel good, but according to how Jesus showed mercy. When something was wrong Jesus showed no mercy! He showed none to the fig tree, but cursed it immediately and then used it as an example.

Mercy is a blessing, so is feeding a hungry man, but misplaced mercy will make him less a person. Godly mercy to the drunk is our blessing, but misplaced mercy cripples him by enabling him. When God wants to deal with a person and we can't seem to deal with it, then our first thought is to show mercy…but then it has indeed become misplaced mercy for we have come between him and God's plan or judgment for his life which might one day change him for mercy can't.

God actually says in Daniel 9:9 that mercy belongs to our God, so when we get into misplaced mercy it is not of

God. *Blessed are the merciful for they shall obtain mercy.* Matthew 5:7.

When my mentor, Dr. Mike Murdock, said, "The future of every relationship is decided by mercy," this was definitely not meaning misplaced mercy, but God's gentle mercy for the deserving!

Show Godly compassion today,
Godly mercy,
not misplaced mercy!!!

CORRECTION

Correction...the path to the better life!

Correction, whether it comes from our God, from within ourselves, or from another—it remains the only path to a better life! Every correction we receive is an improvement in our life! Sometimes it takes us a while to be able to view it in that way.

Correction rubs against our flesh and will eventually kill that flesh if we desire great and better changes in all areas of our life. As long as we live, we are housed in a body of flesh that is opposed to God, therefore opposed to the life found in Him. Correction is most always not received with great joy, but if it is received, will produce greater life, greater joy from that day forward because immediately we began to feel the change, the freedom that correction has brought.

When we are serious about life, we know that embracing correction is bringing a life of more freedom! Correction uncovers the ungodliness in us and continually brings us our ever increasing mind of Christ!

Our life is like the onion. Everything good seems to

come in layers, from precept upon precept, line upon line, to correction—and more correction. We never outgrow the process God uses to kill our flesh... if we are desiring to be more like Jesus we continue to change. Each layer of the onion, (layers of flesh), which gets peeled off, hurts and brings us to tears as more truth is released into our hearts and minds from Christ Jesus.

Another layer—some more hurt—some more tears! This is continuous until we reach the core, (like the heart of onions), the heart of our being, which is a different color than the layers that have been peeled off.

Our heart, like the different color of the core of the onion, is unlike the layers that surrounded us to keep us from seeing our own heart. Revealed there now is the core, like the heart of the onion, it contains all that is necessary for producing more life! It draws its strength from the loss of now dead flesh. Just like when the seed onion or bean seed is planted in dirt, contained within that seed is the immediate nourishment for establishment of growth and reproduction of itself.

Correction is a seed for great strength. The more correction we have endured the greater the strength of God is felt and seen in us. That strength is evidenced in our words, our ministry, our spiritual life, our emotions, even our physical walk! Great is the strength that comes from growth. The larger the plant, or tree or whatever it is that is growing, the greater the strength.

The more things we correct the greater our strength shall be! If we are walking in all the light, (correction), that we see and know, then we are becoming greater and greater in strength! There is also sometimes great remorse for we see damage we have done as we walked uncorrected in our flesh. To the tender heart the pain created by realizing our mistakes makes us reliant on faith in God. Faith to believe that all our wrong, Jesus has now made right; all guilt He has washed away and we walk in great strength into a beautiful, new, and promising future filled with the wisdom of God.

Everything we have ever corrected was something that was wrong and hurtful to us! Praise God, correction frees us from mistakes, faults, making us better, bringing us up to more Godly standards!!! Correction is always improvement when it is done in love for love!!!

Correction is proof that we are loved by God and even that person who corrected us!!! We do not correct when we do not care! The word of God tells me that the rod and reproof are the seeds for wisdom! *Poverty and shame shall be to him that refuseth instruction ; but he that regardeth reproof shall be honored*—Proverbs 13:18.

Walk free today in a new and deeper mind of Christ. Your mistakes, your sins have been forgiven you and all guilt and shame has been removed from you as far as the east is from the west! There is no way to ever find it again for the journey from the east to the west is a place of "never meet!" God has already forgotten your mistakes. Why would you take time to remember something that is gone forever?

My mentor, Dr. Murdock has taught me that I know if you are wise or a fool by your reaction to correction!

Be wise today,
submit,
ask God's forgiveness,
forgive yourself,
then march into a glorious tomorrow with me
with great joy and strength!!!

HOPE

Joyful and Confident Expectation

Let me say right here and now that Jesus Christ is our hope. Without Him and what He did for us, this world would not have even lasted this long, I don't think.

Prolonged discouragement is the seed for lost hope. A person who has lost hope is the person who is now despairing. Some people who have fallen into despair have taken their own lives for in despair there is no hope.

It is very hard to reach a person who has lost hope for when he falls into the next step, despair, few will ever listen to God once that happens. Remember that a despairing person is not listening to God if you attempt to minister to this person. They have gone far beyond that. Nothing or nobody matters to them anymore and if they do not have God in them—we could lose them.

Recognize a person losing hope for it will come in stages, and if it has been a long time without any positive results in their life the steps seem to come even faster in losing hope. This person will no longer talk as one with any vision for the future. They will have, or begin to have, a loss of confidence in that thing or person wherein they hoped. They will experience in all of this a loss of a sense of **security** in the situation or place. Then, the last thing is—they lose heart.

A word, an action, a circumstance can set the person off who has been in a place of discouragement for a long time. This is why it is so significant that we listen to people and really hear them. I am not talking about just listening to hear, but listening to hear their heart. This is so significant to know in order to minister to replace despair with hope, and with words to encourage our fellow man! We can bring a man back from the cliff of despair if we can listen and recognize the place where this one is who is losing hope.

I cannot imagine a life without God, for without Him there is no hope for today or tomorrow, or ever seeing heaven. We are living in a time now where many are losing hope. People are losing hope concerning their finances, the government, their health, jobs, religions that are failing, children rebelling, and the list goes on and on.

We have the hope! We are that hope. Jesus is not walking around as a human now, but walking around inside our lives, our hands, our mouths, and feet! These people who need hope need Jesus! *To them God willed to make known what are the riches of His glory of this mystery among the Gentiles; which is Christ in you the hope of glory*—Colossians 1:27! Paul, at the risk of personal danger and loss of comfort fulfills his responsibility of delivering God's mystery!

We are the bride of Christ. We are carrying within us the hope of answers for all questions; the hope for people, for nations. Salvation from all things is inside us, redemption, healing, restoration, and the list goes on! It is Christ in us!!! We have that hope and we need to be ready in and out of season in order to share hope when others are despairing. *But sanctify the Lord God in your hearts and be ready always to give an answer to every man that asketh you a reason for the hope that is in you in meekness and fear*—1 Peter 3:15!

Don't be the one who destroys a man's hope, dampens his enthusiasm!!! Bring cheer and joy and lift faith with expectations by living out the hope each day that lives in us!!! When the world of a person or a nation starts becoming dark with evil and losing hope, our hope will shine with answers and wisdom from heaven giving much hope!

Give someone some hope today that this too can pass! There is a brighter way, it is the hope that is alive and shining bright in us today!!!

Praise the Lord!!!
He reigns in us even now with hope for everyone,
for every nation!

IS IT FAITH?
PART 1

Let's begin with Heb 11:1:
NOW faith is the substance of things hoped for, the evidence of things not seen!

We have many translations of the Word of God. One translation says "Faith is the warranty deed that the thing for which you have fondly hoped for is at last yours!" I like that too! Paul is simply telling us that faith is laying hold of the un-realties of hope and bringing them into the realm of reality! Don't you just love that?

Faith gives us the assurance that we have it! That silences our fears and brings peace and joy! You may hope to have the strength to do some kind of thing, or to go on a particular journey, etc. Then, what does faith say? It says ...*the Lord is the strength of my life, of whom shall I be afraid*?—Psalm 27:1. Faith grows out of the word of God, it comes by hearing and hearing it.—Romans 10:17.

The reason there is so much **power** when our faith is lifted is because faith will ALWAYS say what the word of God says!!! Always! If you doubt and get in unbelief, then you have taken sides with satan, and you gain evil and fear. That, we know is our unbelief and unbelief is always against the word of God! When you do this, God nor His word will work for you for He does no work for the enemy!

To better understand what something is, we need to know what it is not. So what is not faith? It surely is not hope! Hope is just not the same as believing. David said it is now, and Hebrews says it is now: faith is now! If it is not now, it is not faith! Hope is future tense, faith is always now! I have it NOW!!!

Once we know and understand the principles of faith then we become receivers! Faith makes receiving easy from our God! We receive by faith! God offers us gifts that are as easy to receive as me handing you a cup of tea when we understand faith and how it works for us.

There is a great difference in hoping for and believing! Jesus said in Mark 11:24, *Therefore I say to you, whatever things you ask when you pray, BELIEVE that you receive them and YOU WILL HAVE THEM*! You must believe in God for His words and faith to work for you, to get that answer, that response from God! If it's in the future, then it is hope—you have not faith. If you believe that God is going to do it, then you're hoping. If you have faith it says…..HE HAS DONE IT AND IS DOING IT!!!

God did not promise to heal us. *Himself took our infirmities and bore our sickness*, is not a promise! It is a statement of truth, a fact that already happened. 1 Peter 2:24 is not a promise. It is a statement telling us what God gave us, what belongs to us! We cannot wait until we see something to believe it and receive it!!! If we are praying and things don't change, it is us who needs to change.

God is not going to change…
He is the same yesterday, today and forever!!!
Believe Him today!!!

IS IT FAITH?
PART 2

Faith has a tense—PRESENT!

We have been talking about what faith is not in this, "Is it faith" topics. We know that faith is not hope for hope is future tense and faith is now! We cannot be hoping and think we will get answers when really it is only faith that will produce the answers. These are answers God has already given to us long ago, all we have to do is reach by faith and retrieve those answers NOW, believe that we have them and we do!!!

Our hope in God is a blessed hope and we should always know that and remember that, but we must keep hope in its proper place. Hope cannot take the place of faith, neither can faith take the place of hope. Mercy is not the only thing that can be misplaced, we can have misplaced hope.

Knowing Jesus Christ is our blessed hope gives us joy and peace and happiness. However we must never forget that it is future tense. Our faith will not bring Jesus back, our faith does not determine whether He returns or not. We know He is and we are indeed hoping for His return even now. His return is in **the future**, something we hope for.

The prospect of His coming motivates us to live righteously and pure before God, 1 John 3:2-3. Faith will not make this happen. He will come back whether we have faith to believe it or not. Believing you can have what you hope for, "someday," is not faith it is just hope! If it is not now, it is hope and if it is "now" it is faith.

Hope for the future—Faith for today!

Whatever you have been hoping for you need to stop and think, am I hoping for that, or am I walking in faith that says I NOW have that? Faith is not "Someday!" You will never receive from God anything that you cannot have faith for! Faith is an act.

Some may think that the Holy Spirit is just going to suddenly come upon them and force them or something to happen in their life. That is not true. The Holy Spirit never forces anyone or anything. That would not be of God, for the Holy Spirit is gentle, never pushy. So, let's stop just hanging out with people of faith—hanging out at the altar, and start ACTING on what Jesus has said, what He has spoken to us.

Faith is an act, you must make a move, an act for faith to reach the answer and bring it back to you. You must believe that He will do it when you ask, when you believe, right then! He does it then, even if you do not see it for days! It IS done!!!

AND WHATEVER THINGS YOU ASK IN PRAYER, BELIEVING, YOU WILL RECEIVE—Matthew 21:22!!!
WILL….. not Can!!!

Believe today that when you pray for that which you have been just hoping for, is your NOW, and you shall have it!!!

GOD said that...I am just repeating what HE SAID!!!
Receive a miracle today!!!
You will if you believe!!!

PERSEVERENCE

Steady and continued action or belief
usually over a long period and
especially despite difficulties or setbacks.

I write about this because the truth in the heart of the winner is a great desire to succeed! I believe the most important key to success is perseverance. We not only have to know—we must keep running, but we must also know before we even start. Whatever it is in life we start, then we must persevere if we are to succeed.

Some have not counted the cost and when things get a little rough they bail out, slow down or just quit. A true mark of the successful person is the lasting quality of perseverance. When we see or hear of people who have been great successes, then we know they have this lasting quality even in the face of dislike, disapproval, even in hard difficulties.

A worker must persevere if he is to be a success at his job, even keeping it sometimes. Some blame circumstances for lack of perseverance. I say to you, find the right circumstances, but if you can't, then make those circumstances!

There are all kinds of parking places along the road to success, but we don't park there. We can only get refreshed in the shade of the big oaks that we pass as we press on! Temptation will always be present to stop. A winner never stops! We keep going long after we are tired, because to achieve is to endure.

Negative obstacles only strengthen our resolve at times, and help us to see how much better is the goal we have resolved to achieve. No man has ever stumbled over a mountain, he has only stumbled over a small stone. If we look at the prize instead of the stones that we find in our path, or the stones people throw, we will see that perseverance is indeed the greater for it is indeed the key to our success!

The greatest example of perseverance is Jesus as he continued on carrying His cross no matter what was done or said until he reached the greatest victory this world has ever known. It is far better to be a dream in a broken man than the man with no dreams, for he is the dead man.

> *For you have need of steadfast patience and endurance, so you may perform and fully accomplish the will of God, and thus receive and carry away, and enjoy to the full, what is promised*—Hebrews10:36!

So, we see God said we have need of this! He said not only do we need perseverance, but why and how....

> *Therefore then, since we are surrounded by so great a cloud of witnesses, who have borne testimony to the truth, let us strip off and throw aside every encumbrance, unnecessary weight, and that sin that so readily, definitely and clearly, clings to and entangles us; let us run with patient endurance and steady and active persistence the appointed course of the race that is set before*

us— Hebrews 12:1! (Scripture from Amplified Bible)

Isaiah is speaking prophetic words into our lives when he says to us, we will not faint if we are true servants of The Living God! *Those who wait upon the Lord, shall renew their strength; they shall mount up with wings as eagles, they shall run and not be weary, they shall walk and not faint*—Isaiah 40:31. We **continue** to advance as long as we hold tight to the truth of the Word! We win! We then have the overcomers crown! *As for you brethren, do not grow weary in well* doing—2 Thessalonians 3:13.

God made us who persevere a promise too! Galatians 6:9: *And let us not grow weary while doing good, for in due season we shall reap if we do not lose heart*. Don't lose heart today but keep going and instead of losing everything, you will gain everything you started for!!!

Take heart, Today!!!
YOU Will WIN!!!
Keep going!!!

THOUGHT CONTROL

...We have the mind of Christ.
1 Corinthians 2:16

Praise the Lord! When we learn thought control, then we can prevent many wrong actions and words! Wow! What a relief!

The answer brings freedom every time! The answer brings us to new every time! You know something? God did not give us a brain and fling us onto the earth! He is a God of order and He anticipated every single need and weakness we would possess as human beings! If He had made us perfect we would be like God, and we certainly are not!

God gave us the answer to capturing wrong words, wrong actions.....the problem is we simply don't slow down long enough to give God a simple thought when these times arise. If we did we could control those wrong words, wrong actions. This is the KEY, the answer to our thought control, seek God instantly.

A thought is a developing word or idea that originates from the stimulation of one of our five senses and finds its intellectual delivery from our brain. If we can control our five senses of sight, hearing, touch, smell, and taste, then we can control our thought process. "How do I do this?" you say. It is quite simple but takes a while to progress from trying, to actually developing the right habit of control. Then, and only then, can we control our words and actions.

We have to control what we listen to, what we allow our eyes to see, what we touch, hear, smell or taste. We can do this when we have submitted these senses to Jesus. Eve was captured by her senses, then it became a thought, a word, and then sin.

The man who walks in perfect peace here will be the man who is trusting God to help him with these things for God will do it! We are not proving what is good and acceptable and the perfect will of God when we are not renewing our minds (Romans 12:2). We cannot renew our minds by continuing to think the same thoughts. We must change what is challenging us, trying our faith, creating wrong words and wrong actions.

What is it we are doing with our five senses that is creating wrong thoughts, then wrong words and actions? If we allow wrong thoughts, they will not stop there but will produce a dreadful harvest. We can be led of God here if we want to be led of God. If we commit our works to God, that is the work of our hands and our minds, words, and actions, then He said in Proverbs 16:3 that He would establish our thoughts.

We must bring every disobedient thought into obedience to our God, thus developing the mind of Christ! We cannot do it without using the key I just wrote about, slowing down so that we give God a moment to help us take control—again—of our thoughts.

For the weapons of our warfare are not carnal but mighty in God for pulling down of strongholds. Casting down arguments and every high thing that exalts itself against the knowledge of God, bringing every thought into captivity to the obedience of Christ 2—Corinthians 10:4-5.

We try to control our tongue but we cannot, the Word of God tells us that. God must control our tongue, He is the only one who can. This is a strong hold that many must take into captivity. The longer it has been free to be a stronghold, then the longer it will take us to develop the key of slowing down long enough to consult with our God before allowing the thought that brings sorrow to ourselves and to others.

We need to quote the scriptures He has given us to do this. Either one of these I've written will work for they are alive unto our thoughts with **power**! Imagine the mind of Christ dwelling in us and what horizons of great freedom in a new day it will bring!!!

"When you do your best, God will do the rest!" Dr. Mike Murdock, my mentor has given us great advice here and inspiration to just do it! You can change today every way of thinking you have previously developed!

I have faith in God and in you!
Try Him on this…He will work and you will win!!!

CHEERFULNESS

A necessary ingredient in many desirable traits.

Cheerfulness is something that God desires us to have. He told us in several places in His word to be cheerful. I, being a cheerful person, really believe that the cheerful person is actually the one who is living out John 16:33! I really do! I think it is something that God has given us and we have received in His Word that which accounts for cheerfulness.

Cheerful people have the revelation!!! I have explained my cheerfulness to many who did not understand because the circumstances in my life did not appear to call for cheer. God said this:

These things I have spoken to you, that in Me you may have peace. In the world you will have tribulation; but be of good cheer, I have overcome the world—John 16:33.

It is Christ in me, the anointed one, who has overcome the world and those things around me. That leaves me nothing to do but be cheerful for I know that I know, all things are under my feet now and it will be seen that they are under my feet tomorrow! I do not really believe that a person can be cheerful unless they have overcome and got above the circumstances and tribulations that may be theirs today.

If you really believed that every single thing on this earth that was not of God was under your feet, do you think you would be cheerful? Of course you would, so the problem is that we have not really got the revelation of this particular verse. I am not talking about a person who is funny, laughs, and smiles and seems to be a "barrel of fun." I am talking about genuine cheerfulness that when the devil has come in like a flood, this cheerful person will still be exuding an optimistic attitude, creating a pleasant environment that creates a gladness in the hearts of others. A cheerful person will dispel gloom and despair.

God said He loves a cheerful giver. Why do you think He loves a cheerful giver? He knows He overcame greed for us, so He knows they have overcome also and He loves that quality of Himself in a person. The person who can give and be cheerful because again, it shows us John 16:33!

The person who is cheerful is one of humor, good spirits and full of joy! It shows too! You can't hide real cheerfulness. The person who is carrying it will bring it into every place they come into. Again, I am speaking of real and genuine cheerfulness that comes from the oil of gladness and a great optimistic outlook for a wonderful future.

You will not find a cheerful person seeking or keeping company with someone of poor attitude and negative outlook for life. The two are enemies in the spirit world. One cannot withstand the other. A person of great faith is most always a cheerful person. The cheerful person isn't always getting mad, sulking, and being sullen. The cheerful one is the buoyancy one to our life, our spirit, inspiring with their sunny and upbeat attitude about life and its circumstances.

Cheerfulness is characterized by expressive goodness!!! Cheerfulness reflects willingness, and I believe that is why, as my mentor teaches, that "King Solomon always hired happy people." I think they were cheerful people. The cheerful person comes into a situation and just by his nature and appearance, creates happiness for others.

If we could ever grasp that God is good and He is in us and He has overcome ALL that we face or encounter…..He said, "It is finished!" But, when will we really believe it? That is our seed for cheerfulness! There is nothing according to the Word of God—and He cannot lie—that has the ability to steal our cheer, for He has already overcome it ALL!!!

So today…know this…we can believe it, receive it, and
instead of living fearful, and tearful,
we can live cheerful….
every single day, starting today!!!
Yes!!!

PRESUMING

Believing something for which there is no absolute proof.

Since a lot of people are only presuming and what they are believing is not proven, I think this could be an interesting subject. We are presuming when we have no facts upon which to base our belief. If we take an idea as true only on the basis of probability then it is a presumption.

Some people have religious beliefs, even Christian-like beliefs, yet if asked the facts about what or why they are believing it, they would find they have been presuming.

Old timers used to say, "it pays to know the facts!" This is so true. If we do not know something to be a fact we should not hold it as a belief nor pass it on as a truth. Otherwise we are presuming, and this leads people into presuming, for they too then, are believing something that is not a proven fact.

When we take things for granted, we begin outstepping our bounds, and we are described as forward, or effrontery towards a person or people. A person who presumes he can visit another person without calling is presuming. If a man puts his hands on a woman even in a gesture of friendship he is presuming if she has not indicated or established this is what she wants to happen. Taking a picture of someone you vaguely know is a presumption, if permission has not been granted. Public display of another's picture without their permission will tell us that person is presumptuous.

A gift can be from someone who is presuming when they don't know if it is inappropriate. They have not asked to see what is appropriate. Receiving that gift then is as bad and inappropriate as the giving was. An example of this would be giving a man of God a personal gift when he is not a boyfriend or related. This is presuming.

A neighbor or friend giving a child something without checking with the parents is presuming. Most people who are presumptuous are considered arrogant, disrespectful, and most always transgress the limits of what is permitted or what is appropriate. They consider themselves humble, but in fact, we are terribly prideful when we do this.

There are many things about which we can be presumptuous. Presuming is a boldly arrogant or offensive behavior which the other person not only recognizes but greatly dislikes. If you "just do" things without any thought of whether it is appropriate or not you are presuming.

Everyone has boundaries, and if we cross the wrong boundary we may be scolded, some have even been slapped. We have heard or may have known a man to exhibit the trait of presuming and he was slapped, or asked to leave. He probably never considered this word in his entire life, but just learned one lesson about one person, or one place.

Cutting across a lawn rather than using the sidewalk is presuming that it is not a problem when the person who lives in that house may be very upset with the one who did it. A good rule of thumb here is if there is one single question, then don't do it until you know what is truth or acceptable. Many, many people have done many things all their lives in presuming and never knew it was why they were so disliked.

Women are presuming, just as bad as any man. We don't get off the hook here either. We presume when we sit down in the wrong place, uninvited, walk into rooms, uninvited, and indulge in wrong timing. Since I am a female writing this I will tell you for a fact that there are lots of men who seldom show women the respect they demand themselves. Most women won't tell them, but that is why men are treated with disrespect and dishonor many times, and the men may never know. I'm talking to **single men** here especially, for when married that boundary saves them many times. Laugh out loud here if you want to, its true!

Men, your boundaries for just being a man alone may be much greater than you have been acting like they are. Maybe it would do men and women good to get some facts about a godly woman (or a godly man), the people, and places around them, before they show great dishonor and disrespect by presuming they know the right way to do something, or the right thing to speak.

Just remember if you don't ask for the facts, the truth, then you are presuming and presuming is a great sin for it is birthed from pride.

And whosoever shall exalt himself shall be abased; and he that shall humble himself shall be exalted.
Matthew 23:12

FRUIT OR NUTS

Spirit or Flesh

Galatians 5:22-23: *But the fruit of the Spirit is love, joy, peace, longsuffering, kindness, goodness, faithfulness, gentleness and self control against which there is no law*!

These virtues are characterized as fruit in contrast to "works." The only way our life will produce this fruit is by a seasoned walk with the Holy Spirit. We can do none of these through our own efforts. A person may appear to have fruit, but after close inspection we find it is not real fruit.

Realize that the "works" of the flesh is plural, different from the "fruit" of the spirit which we see is singular. That is because the fruit is one and cannot be divided. When a man or woman of God is controlled by the Holy Spirit then He will produce ALL of these beautiful graces. God is such a God of order—order in the sequence of the ten commandments, order to the sequence of His words in The Lord's Prayer. There is order in His orchard of fruit too!!!

The first three attributes of the fruit of the Spirit deal

with our attitude towards God, the second three deal with our social life and our relationships. Then, of course, the other three deal with principles that guide a Christians conduct here on earth.

We cannot judge people, but as someone has said, we can certainly be a fruit inspector. This is how we will know if a person is controlled by the Holy Spirit! *But we have the mind of Christ*—1 Corinthians 2:16.

We need to grow some fruit! If we do not grow fruit, Jesus will cut us down for we are useless as His children on this earth without fruit! Many are hungry and we must be able to extend fruit to them, for them to see real food, real fruit! They partake of the fruit of the Spirit through its demonstration in our lives.

May your branches sag to the ground under the weight of great and luscious fruit!

WORKS OF THE FLESH

A dark subject that sheds great light for change.

Galatians 5:19-21, tells us exactly what Paul made clear was works of the flesh.

> Now the works of the flesh are manifest, which are these, adultery, fornication, uncleanness, lasciviousness, idolatry, witchcraft, hatred, variance, emulations, wrath, strife, seditions, heresies. envyings, murder, drunkenness, revellings, and such like of which I tell you before as I have told you in time past, that they which do such things shall not inherit the kingdom of God.

People who do these things are not led by the Holy Spirit. The person who is led by the Holy Spirit is not under these bondages and condemnation. The works of the flesh could be grouped as sexual sins, in verse 19 and sins connected with pagan religions, the first two of verse 20 and then the sins of temper which are the next nine, and then the last two are sins of drunkenness.

My advice to anyone who wants to live a purified and cleansed life is verses 16-18 of this same chapter.

I say then, walk in the Spirit, and you shall not fulfill the lust of the flesh, for the flesh lusts against the Spirit and the Spirit against the flesh; and these are contrary to one another, so that you do not do the things that you wish. But if you are led by the Spirit, you are not under the law.

It is very obvious here that we cannot live this kind of holy life without the help of the Holy Spirit. Tell the Holy Spirit you want Him to lead you today! Surrender your will to Him so that you are lead each day by His power and not by your might!

There—you will find a very rewarding life!!!

INCREASE

Gain—Grow—Produce

Increase is something that we cannot avoid! It makes no difference whether we are living righteously or sinfully, we are increasing in it! You might say, "Well, how is that?" My mentor, Dr. Mike Murdock teaches us that, "We are a walking warehouse of seeds." Everything we do, everything we say, everything we are not doing, everything we are not saying, everything we are giving and everything we are not giving—everything, even hoarding...are all seeds!

We know from planting a simple **bean seed** or watermelon seed that we are going to harvest more than we planted; more than we sowed every single time! Every time the enemy tries to tell us we are losing, every time he tells us that we can't do something, tries to defeat us, then we need to quote the word to him. *And Jesus increased in wisdom and statute and in favor with God and man*—Luke 2:52, and HE never changes.

He is still increasing today, but today He is increasing in us. *To whom God would make known what is the riches of the glory of this mystery among the Gentiles; which is*

Christ in you the hope of glory—Colossians 1:27. Christ Jesus lives in us and so we are increasing in everything in every way with every seed every single day!!! Even the power of our seeds is steadily increasing! Yes!!!

This is just another reason we need to be living a holy and righteous life before our God, for even the wrong in our life is a seed and will increase. For instance jealousy and anger are seeds that increase and bring murder one day, or increases until it has murdered our health, if not forsaken.

The word says that wisdom can increase until it becomes a grief, and knowledge until it becomes increased sorrow. I believe that is why Jesus was crying over Jerusalem. He saw their destination when they would not let Him gather them because Wisdom itself told Him of their future.

2 Corinthians talks about an increased faith. David tells us that the earth will yield her increase when God's people praise Him. Praise is the seed for the earth itself to increase her yield, and God's increase of blessings on our lives too!

Psalm 67:5-7: *Of his government God said there would be increase without end*!!!

When we sow faithfully through our righteous decisions, then God said He would give the increase!!! He is a God of increase! There are some words that are not in His vocabulary, not found in any place in His words to us either. It is because He has a creative tongue and every word He speaks has an assignment and that assignment is performed for it increases and never returns void!!!

Nowhere in His Word does God ever speak of decrease, de-escalating, diminishing, downsizing, dwindling, lowering, reducing or anything else that is subtraction or has anything to do with subtraction. All of that is reserved for sin, the devil, and all his angels. That is what satan does. God cannot give us something that He does not have!!!

In Acts chapter 9 we find that Saul increased in strength until he became a man that confounded his enemies. God changed him and his weakness became his strength! He increased after having an encounter with The Living God!!! We must increase for we are the sons of God, it is in our DNA to increase. It is impossible for us to do anything but increase!!!

The question is…what are we increasing in….is it the same as with Jesus? He increased in favor with God and man! We can too, and become bigger and better every single day of our lives even into the forever!!!

We have not yet become ALL that we can become
for we are ever increasing!!!

THE WEAKER VESSEL

Men, this is directed at you as God also directed a word to us about this very thing. Let's read it:

Husbands, likewise, dwell with them with understanding, giving honor to the wife as to the weaker vessel, and as being heirs together of the grace of life, that your prayers may not be hindered—1Peter 3:7

Men this is an instruction which carries a great warning! You must carry out this instruction for God to answer your prayers! He is serious! He knows how He created the woman, the weaker vessel.

Men…do you really know your wives? Do you really know what it means to dwell with her as the weaker vessel? What exactly does this mean? It does not mean that she is not all she can be. But all that she is, is still not as strong as a man! This concerns not just the physical, but the emotional as well. An example of this is when a son, a brother, a husband, or father who must be the bearer of bad news to a daughter, wife, sister, or mother. They will say, "Let me tell her." They are trying to protect this weaker vessel. This is a person who understands that it is going to be something hard, something too hard to present without love and understanding.

A man may do this without realizing he is actually recognizing she is not as strong as he is or as strong as others may think she is. Maybe she won't be able to handle this information. "So how," you may ask, "does a man incorporate this into his everyday life with his Godmate as God instructed him?"

First of all he must recognize she is not as strong as he, and she never will be. In the beginning you should find her to be much more sensitive than you are. Things that do not bother you may bother her, maybe even irritate her. What you may be capable of ignoring she may not be able to, for she is not as strong as you are in her emotional make up. It is very important that a man knows what he does and/or doesn't do that his Godmate may find upsetting. When he knows these things, to continue on without changing or discussing the matter is not only handling his wife's life carelessly, but also acting very carelessly and/or talking in a way that is not loving and thoughtful. Perhaps this is where the old saying applies that the man is the head of the home, but the wife is the neck that moves that head!

Let me give you an example. If you are a man and you watch a sporting event consistently while putting it ahead of your wife's wishes concerning her home and family, this can lead to problems. She may be polite and kindly suggest that you need to plan more wisely in that area. If you continue, she will mention it again, maybe talking with you about it. But one day she may become angry.

Her emotions have been touched for her home is her heart—her family is her heart. She is now angry because her emotional feelings have been dishonored, and ignored. Not so much because of what you are doing, but because you have ignored her deep feelings. She now feels like a "second fiddle" to the sport and a second rate person in your life.

Another example could be a person who she has discerned as an enemy of her home or her life. She has let you know this. You may see no enemy, but you must recognize her feelings, her emotions about these different things. I hope it goes no further than "the dog house!" Maybe you are in "the doghouse" and don't even know why. ASK why! (I hope your wife is emotionally honest.)

A wife is all about emotions much unlike the man! Some men, especially those who do not understand their wives, do not feel comfortable at these times. A husband can be very successful in these areas. He just needs to apply understanding and listen. He must know what upsets his wife! He must avoid these areas completely for him to see great peace within himself. Ask her:

- What makes her angry?
- What is it she does not like?
- What makes her upset?
- What makes her feel insecure?
- How can you help her understand your feelings and needs?
- How can you be a strength to her?

When a man knows the answers to these questions and has taken the opportunity to calmly express his feelings and needs to her, it is up to both of them to work out the details with the needs of the family as top priority for their time together. Everyone's circumstance will be different, of course, depending upon many factors. For instance, if the wife does not work outside the home, she can make certain concessions that one with an outside job could not.

Marriage is a covenantal partnership and, as all partnerships, requires diplomacy and consideration. It is not just one person giving up everything so the other can be happy—believe me, you will not be. It is supposed to be a melding of two lives for mutual benefit in life and in Kingdom building.

You can do this.
Take this
and
RUN WITH IT!

ABOUT THE AUTHOR

RACHEL

Rachel received the call from the Lord to move to Texas in February, 2004, from Greensboro N.C. Since being in Texas, God has used her in many individual lives, groups, and churches. God raised Rachel up as a warrior, one of His end-time messengers in His army for such a time as this.

She has served in many capacities in the church, starting intercessory prayer in the churches where God sent her. She also served as leader/co-coordinator in her home church raising up 18 women into their ministry and destinies. Rachel is a woman of God, like unto a flame of fire, divinely taught by the Holy Spirit. She speaks to the heart, bringing revelation of the Son of man, Christ Jesus.

> Joel 2:3: *A fire devours before them and behind them a flame burns.*

Her message of repentance is of the same spirit of John the Baptist; spoken with **power** and boldness to lead His bride to conviction and purity.

> Hebrews 4:12: *For the Word of God is quick and sharper than any two edged sword piercing even to the dividing asunder of soul and spirit and of the joints and marrow and is a discerner of the thoughts and intents of the heart.*

Rachel is blessed with a strong prophetic anointing, word of knowledge, and healing with creative miracles. She is a fearless warrior of intercession, with a special anointing for restoration of finances as well as family restorations.